LOVING-KINDNESS IN PLAIN ENGLISH

LOVING-KINDNESS
IN PLAIN ENGLISH

The Practice of
METTA

Bhante Gunaratana

Wisdom Publications
199 Elm Street
Somerville, MA 02144 USA
wisdomexperience.org

Library of Congress Cataloging-in-Publication Data
Names: Gunaratana, Henepola, 1927– author.
Title: Metta : loving-kindness in plain English / Bhante Henepola Gunaratana.
Description: Somerville, MA : Wisdom Publications, 2017. | Includes index.
Identifiers: LCCN 2016024819 (print) | LCCN 2016045832 (ebook) | ISBN
   9781614292494 (pbk. : alk. paper) | ISBN 1614292493 (pbk. : alk. paper) |
   ISBN 9781614292647 ()
Subjects: LCSH: Compassion—Religious aspects—Buddhism.
Classification: LCC BQ4360 .G86 2017 (print) | LCC BQ4360 (ebook) | DDC
   294.3/5—dc23
LC record available at https://lccn.loc.gov/2016024819

ISBN 978-1-61429-249-4   ebook ISBN 978-1-61429-264-7

25 24 23 22
5 4 3 2

Cover design by Gopa & Ted2, Inc. Set in Fairfield LH Light 11/16.

Printed in the United States of America.

Please visit fscus.org.

Contents

Preface

Even though there are several books on metta, or loving-friendliness, this Plain English book is based primarily on the famous *Discourse on Loving-Friendliness*. Known as the *Karaniya Metta Sutta* in Pali, or just *Metta Sutta* for short, this discourse is recited more often than any other discourse, on all occasions in Theravada Buddhist countries. As we so often recite this discourse, we thought writing a book elucidating the meaning of this profound sutta would benefit those who are not quite familiar with the Pali language in which we recite this discourse most of the time.

I am very grateful to Judy Larson and Gyula Nagy for their kind assistance in preparing this book. Also I am grateful to Wisdom Publications for their high-quality work in making this book available to the public interested in practicing loving-friendliness meditation. Last but not least, I thank Josh Bartok, Arnie Kotler, and Brianna Quick for the final polishing of this book.

With Metta,
Bhante Gunaratana
Bhavana Society Forest Monastery
and Meditation Center

CHAPTER 1

Metta: Our Natural State

*L*oving-kindness" is the most common translation of the Pali word *metta*—and it's a major component of Buddhist practice. The teachings of the Buddha were transmitted orally from generation to generation for nearly five centuries before monks in Sri Lanka wrote them down in 29 B.C.E. in the Pali language. The word *metta* is derived from another word, *mitta*, which means "friend." *Mitta* also means "sun." We depend on the sun's warmth to survive, and we rely on loving friendship to thrive. Accordingly, my own preferred translation of *metta* is "loving-friendliness"—and that's the term I mostly use throughout the rest of this book.

Each year during his forty-five-year teaching career, the Buddha led a three-month retreat during India's rainy season. Monastics from all over the country came to the Jeta Grove, which had been gifted to him by his generous supporter, Anathapindika, to meditate together with the Buddha. On one occasion, he asked sixty of the monks to go to a remote forest and practice meditations there.

When the monks arrived, nearby villagers built huts for them, but the forest's spirits (the story goes) weren't happy to have their lives interrupted by these men. Instead of welcoming them, the spirits conjured ghostlike images near the footpaths and scattered corpses throughout the forest to frighten them away. Seeing the ghosts and smelling rotting flesh, many monks fell ill. And so they all went back to the Jeta Grove to ask the Buddha what to do.

After they described their experience, the Buddha encouraged them to return to the forest. "You went without a weapon," he told them. "This time you'll need to be armed." Then he gave them a "weapon"— the *Discourse on Loving-Friendliness* (*Karaniya Metta Sutta*, or *Metta Sutta* for short)—and advised them to recite it eight times each month.

The monks went back to the forest and began reciting the *Metta Sutta* twice weekly. The spirits were transformed, and instead of causing trouble, they began protecting the monks from the dangers of the forest. Villagers continued to offer patronage, feeling especially appreciative of the monks' peaceful demeanors and kindness. The practice of loving-friendliness offers us protection.

The Buddha taught practices for the cultivation of loving-friendliness. These entail sending loving energy inward, then outward, while reciting certain phrases such as "May I be happy," and "May all beings be happy"—but these are not mere wishful thoughts. They are part of a practice that can truly transform your heart—and your brain! Research shows that loving-friendliness meditation has significant benefits ranging from enhanced well-being to relief from illness and improved emotional intelligence.

Metta is not ordinary love. It is the quality of love we experience in our whole being, a love that has no ulterior motive—and no opposite. It can never become hatred; the love-hate dichotomy simply does not apply. When we say that we love such-and-such a person or thing, we usually mean that his or her appearance, behavior, ideas, or attitudes fill a perceived deficiency in us. We don't actually see the other person. If their traits change, we might no longer feel love. When our tastes, whims, or fancies change, we might also fall out of love. We love now, but perhaps later we'll hate. We love when everything is smooth and easy, but we may feel the opposite when things get difficult. When our love is that situational, what we call "love" is not metta, but lust, greed, or even exploitation.

One American *vipassana* teacher, Joseph Goldstein, explains metta this way:

> This kind of love has many qualities that distinguish it from other more usual experiences of love mixed with a desire or attachment. Born of great generosity, metta is caring and kindness that does not seek self-benefit. It does not look for anything in return or by way of exchange: "I will love you if you love me," or "I will love you if you behave in a certain way." Because loving-kindness is never associated with anything harmful, it always arises from a purity of heart.

This purity of heart that allows us to feel a warm-hearted friendliness to all beings is natural to us. When we cultivate loving-friendliness, we are simply allowing our innate generosity to grow and flourish.

When I was eight years old, I lost my night vision, probably because of malnutrition. After dark, it was as if I were blind. I couldn't see anything at all, even with the light from a kerosene lamp. My brothers and sisters teased me about it, saying I was pretending, but my mother was quite concerned. She consulted the village medicine man, who gave her a bitter-tasting potion for me. It was made from an herb, but he wouldn't tell her its name. Many people in Sri Lanka believed herbal medicines had mystical powers, and their components were often kept secret.

My mother was supposed to grind the herb into a paste and feed it to me every day until my eyesight improved. The paste tasted wretched, and to make matters worse, I was supposed to take this foul concoction early in the morning, when my stomach was empty. To get me to take that medicine, my mother used the power of love.

Before anyone else in the house was awake, she would take me onto her lap, hug me, kiss me, and tell me stories in a low whisper. After a few minutes, I was so relaxed and happy that I would have done anything she asked. That was the moment she would put the medicine in my mouth and tell me to swallow it quickly. She always mixed the bitter paste with sugar, though it still tasted awful. After several months of that daily ritual, I completely recovered my eyesight.

Now, many years later, I understand the power of loving-friendliness. It helps us swallow the bitterness of life.

The Buddha used the power of metta to "conquer" many of his enemies. In one story, the Buddha was returning from his alms round with his retinue of monks when his evil and ambitious cousin, Devadatta, let loose a fierce elephant. As the massive mammal rushed toward the Buddha, trumpeting aggressively, the Buddha projected thoughts of metta toward it. Ananda, the Buddha's attendant, ran in front of the Buddha to shield him, but the Buddha asked him to step aside, knowing the projection of love would be sufficient. The impact of the Buddha's metta radiation was immediate and overwhelming. By the time the elephant neared the Buddha, it had been completely tamed and knelt before him respectfully.

Loving-friendliness is a natural faculty concealed beneath our greed, hatred, and delusion. It is cultivated through wisdom and mindfulness. No one can grant it to us. We have to find it in ourselves and cultivate it mindfully. When the ego gets out of the way, loving-friendliness arises naturally. Joseph Goldstein adds, "Metta does not make distinctions among beings. It embraces all; there is no one who falls outside of its domain."

Loving-friendliness is a warm wash of fellow-feeling, a sense of interconnectedness with all beings. Because we wish for peace, happiness, and joy for ourselves, we know that all beings must wish for these qualities. Loving-friendliness radiates to the whole world the wish that all beings enjoy a comfortable life with harmony, mutual appreciation, and appropriate abundance.

Though we all have the seed of loving-friendliness within us, we must make the effort to cultivate it. When we are rigid, uptight, tense, anxious, and full of worries and fears, our natural capacity for loving-friendliness cannot flourish. To nurture the seed of loving-friendliness, we must learn to relax. In a peaceful state of mind, such as we get from mindfulness meditation, we can forget our past differences with others and forgive their faults, weaknesses, and offenses. Then loving-friendliness naturally grows within us.

Loving-friendliness begins with a thought. Typically our minds are full of views, opinions, beliefs, ideas. We have been conditioned by our culture, traditions, education, associations, and experiences. From these mental conditions, we have developed prejudices and judgments. These rigid ideas stifle our natural loving-friendliness.

Yet within this tangle of confused thinking, the idea of our warm and friendly interconnection with others does occasionally come up. We catch a glimpse of it as we might glimpse a tree during a flash of lightning. As we learn to relax and let go of negativity, we begin to recognize our biases and not let them dominate our minds. Then the thought of loving-friendliness begins to shine, showing its true strength and beauty.

As I've said, the loving-friendliness that we wish to cultivate is not love as we ordinarily understand it. When you say you love someone, what you conceive in your mind is generally an emotion conditioned by the behavior or qualities of that person. Perhaps you admire the person's appearance, manner, ideas, voice, or attitude. Yet should these conditions change, or your tastes, whims, and fancies change, what you call love might change as well. In extreme cases, this kind of dualistic love is related to hate. You may love one person and hate another. Or you love someone now and hate them later. Or you love whenever you feel like it and not when you don't. Or you love when everything is smooth and rosy and hate when anything goes wrong.

If your love changes from time to time, place to place, and situation to situation in this fashion, that which you call love is not what the Buddha taught, not the skillful thought of loving-friendliness. It may be lust, greed for material security, desire to feel loved, or some other form of greed in disguise. True loving-friendliness has no ulterior motive. It never changes into hate as circumstances change. It never makes you angry if you do not get favors in return. Loving-friendliness motivates you to behave kindly to all beings at all times and to speak gently in their presence and in their absence.

When it has fully matured, your net of loving-friendliness embraces everything in the universe without exception. It has no limitations, no boundaries. Your thought of loving-friendliness includes not only all beings as they are at this moment, but also your wish that all of them, without any discrimination or favoritism, will be happy in the limitless future.

CHAPTER 2

Meditations on Loving-Friendliness

W̶e *are* loving-friendliness. Metta is the nature of the universe and the true nature of each of us. To clear greed, hatred, and delusion from the field of our consciousness and allow our basic nature to arise, we need only allow good wishes to flow. The Buddha offered us some tools with which to do that.

Yet metta recitations are not magic formulas. They don't work by themselves. If you practice, truly participating in each statement and investing them with your own energy, they will be transformative. Generally, when we send out thoughts of loving-friendliness, compassion, appreciative joy, and equanimity to others, our own hearts and minds are naturally and effortlessly filled with those qualities. Our own thoughts of anger and greed also naturally fade away when these feelings take root in our mind. I hope you will try these practices, which I discuss below. And when you do try them, I hope you will see their power for yourself.

In recent years, scientists at Stanford, the University of Wisconsin, and many other institutions have studied the results of metta meditation. One study found that practicing loving-friendliness meditation increases love, joy, contentment, gratitude, hope, interest, amusement, and awe. These positive emotions then produce increases in a wide range of personal resources, such as mindfulness, purpose, and social support, and decreases in illness, resulting in more satisfaction and less depression.

Loving-friendliness meditation also enhances interpersonal attitudes and emotions and increases helping behavior, social connection, compassion, and empathic responses to others' distress, and
decreases biases. In other studies, loving-friendliness meditation
decreased migraine headaches and lower-back pain, depression,
PTSD, and even schizophrenia-spectrum disorders. Practicing
loving-friendliness regularly activates and strengthens areas of the
brain responsible for empathy and emotional intelligence and even
increases gray-matter volume. In one study, just ten minutes of
metta meditation facilitated entry into a relaxing, restorative state
and increased anti-aging markers.

Other studies show that loving-friendliness meditation reduces
self-criticism and improves self-compassion.

But the Buddha discovered all this more than two and a half mil-
lennia ago.

The Buddha taught us to start the practice by sending loving-
friendliness to ourselves. Then do the same for those closest to us,
and work outward from our own circle of friends until we can project
a flow of metta to those we don't like at all, and finally to all beings.
You can practice anytime. I recommend doing this meditation right
after waking up and again at bedtime. Practicing metta helps you
live on an even keel, sleep well, and wake up energized. As loving-
friendliness develops, your thoughts, words, and deeds become more
meaningful, truthful, pleasant, and beneficial to yourself and others.

SENDING METTA INWARD

We begin the practice by cultivating love for ourselves. When you
love yourself, it is easy and natural to extend that love to others. One
who truly loves himself will not harm others. She who loves herself
will tune in to the energy of loving-friendliness and understand how

magnificent it would be if every heart in the world would share this feeling. One who doesn't love himself cannot truly love another. In the Kosala Samyutta, the Buddha said, "Having traveled all quarters with the mind, one finds none anywhere dearer than oneself. Likewise, each person holds himself most dear. Hence one who loves himself will not harm others." So first and foremost, offer metta to yourself.

The Buddha called greed, hatred, and delusion the three poisons. These difficult states of mind can overtake us. In the *Discourse for Cunda the Silversmith* (*Cunda Kammaraputta Sutta*), the Buddha recommends practicing non-greed, non-hatred, and non-delusion. These practices mean not simply giving up behavior that hurts ourselves and others, but also taking up behavior that benefits ourselves and others. They mean being actively generous and deliberately kind, as well as cultivating wisdom.

Take a moment to think about what it feels like to practice non-greed or non-hatred—how the absence of such feelings makes room in our heart for loving-friendliness. We may begin to understand why the Buddha recommended these practices when we look at what happens in our own experience of them. For example, you may find that while speaking with metta to someone, you feel very happy. Later, when you remember how the other person smiled and shone during the friendly conversation, you feel happy once again. Even planning to do something with metta for someone feels positive—it helps your mind generate endless energy so that you are not as tired as you usually might feel. Being kind to others no longer seems like a chore when it is done with metta. And our cordiality and warm-heartedness uplifts those around us so they feel at ease. Seeing everyone working together in friendliness will bring you tremendous joy. The felt sensation of greed and anger by no means leaves you feeling at ease like this.

Practice metta anonymously with no expectation of reward. When the desire for recognition sneaks in, your metta mind repels it. Similarly, if pride tries to sneak in through the back door, your metta shuts this door. Listen to your heart. Be honest. See how you feel when someone speaks to you with loving-friendliness. No other soothing and comforting thought or feeling can replace metta. It must come from deep wisdom and understanding.

If you are new to meditation, you may find it helpful to practice metta meditation seated in a quiet, comfortable place. At the beginning of each meditation session, inwardly or outwardly recite sentences like these to yourself:

May I be well, happy, and peaceful. May no harm come to me. May no difficulties come to me. May no problems come to me. May I always meet with success. May I also have patience, courage, understanding, and determination to meet and overcome inevitable difficulties, problems, and failures in life.

Really feel the intention. Then recite words like these:

May my mind be filled with the thought of loving-friendliness, compassion, appreciative joy, and equanimity. May I be generous. May I be gentle. May I be grateful. May I be relaxed. May I be happy and peaceful. May I be healthy. May my heart become tender. May my words be pleasing to others.

After truly connecting to those intentions, recite these words:

May all that I see, hear, smell, taste, touch, and think help me cultivate loving-friendliness, compassion, appreciative joy, equanimity, generosity, and gentleness. May my behavior be friendly and my loving-friendliness be a source of peace and happiness. May my behavior help my personality. May I be free from fear, anxiety, worry, and restlessness. Wherever I go, may I meet people with happiness, peace, and friendliness. May I be protected in all directions from greed, anger, aversion, hatred, jealousy, and fear.

Radiating Metta to Those We Love

When we have awakened metta in ourselves, we are ready to send metta to those we love. These people might include parents, teachers, benefactors, relatives, spouses, children, and friends. Of course it is not necessary you recite *exactly* the words that follow, but I offer them here so you can feel their intention and power:

May my parents be well, happy, and peaceful. May no harm come to them. May no difficulties come to them. May no problems come to them. May they always meet with success. May they also have patience, courage, understanding, and determination to meet and overcome inevitable difficulties, problems, and failures in life.

May my parents' minds be filled with the thought of loving-friendliness, compassion, appreciative joy, and equanimity. May they be generous. May they be gentle. May they be grateful. May they be relaxed. May they be happy and peaceful. May they be healthy. May their hearts become soft. May their words be pleasing to others.

May all that my parents see, hear, smell, taste, touch, and think help them cultivate loving-friendliness, compassion, appreciative joy, equanimity, generosity, and gentleness. May their behavior be friendly and their loving-friendliness be a source of peace and happiness. May this behavior help their personalities. May they be free from fear, tension, anxiety, worry, and restlessness.

Wherever they go in the world, may they meet people with happiness, peace, and friendliness. May they be protected in all directions from greed, anger, aversion, hatred, jealousy, and fear.

May my teachers be well, happy, and peaceful. May no harm come to them. May no difficulties come to them. May no problems come to them. May they always meet with success. May they also have patience, courage, understanding, and determination to meet and overcome inevitable difficulties, problems, and failures in life.

May my teachers' minds be filled with the thought of loving-friendliness, compassion, appreciative joy, and equanimity. May they be generous. May they be gentle. May they be grateful. May they be relaxed. May they be happy and peaceful. May they be healthy. May their hearts become soft. May their words be pleasing to others.

May all that my teachers see, hear, smell, taste, touch, and think help them to cultivate loving-friendliness, compassion, appreciative joy, equanimity, generosity, and gentleness. May their behavior be friendly and their loving-friendliness be a source of peace and happiness. May this behavior help their personalities. May all of them be free from fear, tension, anxiety, worry, and restlessness.

Wherever they go in the world, may they meet people with happiness, peace, and friendliness. May they be protected in all directions from greed, anger, aversion, hatred, jealousy, and fear.

May my relatives be well, happy, and peaceful. May no harm come to them. May no difficulties come to them. May no problems come to them. May they always meet with success. May they also have patience, courage, understanding, and determination to meet and overcome inevitable difficulties, problems, and failures in life.

May my relatives' minds be filled with the thought of loving-friendliness, compassion, appreciative joy, and equanimity. May they be generous. May they be gentle. May they be grateful. May they be relaxed. May they be happy and peaceful. May they be healthy. May their hearts become soft. May their words be pleasing to others.

May all that my relatives see, hear, smell, taste, touch, and think help them to cultivate loving-friendliness, compassion, appreciative joy, equanimity, generosity, and gentleness. May their behavior be friendly and their loving-friendliness be a source of peace and happiness. May this behavior help their personalities. May all of them be free from fear, tension, anxiety, worry, and restlessness.

Wherever they go in the world, may they meet people with happiness, peace, and friendliness. May they be protected in all directions from greed, anger, aversion, hatred, jealousy, and fear.

May my friends be well, happy, and peaceful. May no harm come to them. May no difficulties come to them. May no problems come to them. May they always meet with success. May they also have patience, courage, understanding, and determination to meet and overcome inevitable difficulties, problems, and failures in life.

May my friends' minds be filled with the thought of loving-friendliness, compassion, appreciative joy, and equanimity. May they be generous. May they be gentle. May they be grateful. May they be relaxed. May they be happy and peaceful. May they be healthy. May their hearts become soft. May their words be pleasing to others.

May all that my friends see, hear, smell, taste, touch, and think help them to cultivate loving-friendliness, compassion, appreciative joy, equanimity, generosity, and gentleness. May their behavior be friendly and their loving-friendliness be a source of peace and happiness. May this behavior help their personalities. May all of them be free from fear, tension, anxiety, worry, and restlessness.

Wherever they go in the world, may they meet people with happiness, peace, and friendliness. May they be protected in all directions from greed, anger, aversion, hatred, jealousy, and fear.

RADIATING METTA TO NEUTRAL BEINGS

The largest category of beings is those we don't have strong feelings for one way or the other. After radiating metta to those we love, we are ready to send loving-friendliness to those about whom our feelings could be described as neutral, people we don't usually think about at all. Here's what that those recitations look like:

May all neutral persons be well, happy, and peaceful. May no harm come to them. May no difficulties come to them. May no problems come to them. May they always meet with success. May they also have patience, courage, understanding, and determination to meet and overcome inevitable difficulties, problems, and failures in life.

May all neutral persons' minds be filled with the thought of loving-friendliness, compassion, appreciative joy, and equanimity. May they be generous. May they be gentle. May they be grateful. May they be relaxed. May they be happy and peaceful. May they be healthy. May their hearts become soft. May their words be pleasing to others.

May everything that all neutral persons see, hear, smell, taste, touch, and think help them to cultivate loving-friendliness, compassion, appreciative joy, equanimity, generosity, and gentleness. May their behavior be friendly and their loving-friendliness be a source of peace and happiness. May this behavior help their personalities. May all of them be free from fear, tension, anxiety, worry, and restlessness.

Wherever they go in the world, may they meet people with happiness, peace, and friendliness. May they be protected in all directions from greed, anger, aversion, hatred, jealousy, and fear.

SENDING LOVING-FRIENDLINESS TO A DIFFICULT PERSON

The fourth category of those to whom we send our love is adversaries, those we have conflicts with or feelings of ill will toward. Why send loving-friendliness to your enemies? The reason is simple. If your enemies are well, happy, and peaceful, they won't be your enemies! If they are free from problems, pain, suffering, affliction, neurosis, psychosis, paranoia, fear, tension, or anxiety, they won't cause you harm. Sending loving-friendliness to your enemies is a practical exercise. If you can help them overcome their problems simply by sending them love, you both can live in peace and happiness.

In each step of the practice, cultivate loving-friendliness for the purification of your own mind. As you do so, you become friendly, without biases, prejudices, discrimination, or hatred. This noble behavior allows you to help others reduce their own pain and suffering. Compassionate people can help others. Those without loving-friendliness cannot. Loving behavior includes thought, speech, and action. Therefore it is more pleasant for us to cultivate the noble thought "May all beings be happy" than to think, "I despise him." A noble thought can manifest in noble behavior.

Here are the recitations for sending metta to those troubling us:

May my enemies be well, happy, and peaceful. May no harm come to them. May no difficulties come to them. May no problems come to them. May they always meet with success. May they also have patience, courage, understanding, and determination to meet and overcome inevitable difficulties, problems, and failures in life.

May all unfriendly persons' minds be filled with the thought of loving-friendliness, compassion, appreciative joy, and equanimity. May they be generous. May they be gentle. May they be grateful. May they be relaxed. May they be happy and peaceful. May they be healthy. May their hearts become soft. May their words be pleasing to others.

May everything that all unfriendly persons see, hear, smell, taste, touch, and think help them to cultivate loving-friendliness, compassion, appreciative joy, equanimity, generosity, and gentleness. May their behavior be friendly and their loving-friendliness be a source of peace and happiness. May this behavior help their personalities. May all of them be free from fear, tension, anxiety, worry, and restlessness.

Wherever they go in the world, may they meet people with happiness, peace, and friendliness. May they be protected in all directions from greed, anger, aversion, hatred, jealousy, and fear.

RADIATING LOVE TO ALL BEINGS

Close your eyes and envision the whole universe—the earth, the stars, everything you've ever experienced or thought, every being you've ever met, and all those you will never meet. Breathe calmly and allow loving-friendliness to arise within you. When you feel it, send this loving energy to all beings in the universe. The purpose of sending metta forth in the six directions—north, south, east, west, above, and below—is so our minds will experience pure, warm loving-friendliness.

When we envision particular individuals, we can get emotionally involved. If we like certain people, our mind might arouse attachment. The thought of losing someone to whom we feel attached contracts us. Fear can arise and our heart closes. When we envision those we don't like, resentments can arise, also causing contraction. Sending loving-friendliness in all directions, radiating the loving-friendliness in us toward all beings, can be a heart-opening purification.

Here are the recitations for this part of the practice:

May all beings be well, happy, and peaceful. May no harm come to them. May no difficulties come to them. May no problems come to them. May they always meet with success. May they also have patience, courage, understanding, and determination to meet and overcome inevitable difficulties, problems, and failures in life.

May all beings' minds be filled with the thought of loving-friendliness, compassion, appreciative joy, and equanimity. May they be generous. May they be gentle. May they be grateful. May they be relaxed. May they be happy and peaceful. May they be healthy. May their hearts become soft. May their words be pleasing to others.

May everything that all beings see, hear, smell, taste, touch, and think help them to cultivate loving-friendliness, compassion, appreciative joy, equanimity, generosity, and gentleness. May their behavior be friendly and their loving-friendliness be a source of peace and happiness. May this behavior help their personalities. May all of them be free from fear, tension, anxiety, worry, and restlessness.

Wherever they go in the world, may they meet people with happiness, peace, and friendliness. May they be protected in all directions from greed, anger, aversion, hatred, jealousy, and fear.

Stay with the feeling of loving-friendliness. Explore the physical and mental feelings associated with metta recitation. Now drop the words and stay with the feeling. Radiate the pure feeling of loving-friendliness to the whole universe.

This practice is not limited to a particular region, village, or country. We send our metta toward the whole wide world. The practice goes beyond boundaries. When we say, "May God bless my family, my village, or my nation," we limit our practice of metta. Normally, we aren't concerned with what happens to other families, villages, or countries. These are tribal instincts, elements in our primitive brain that reinforce the boundaries between us. Armies invade others' territories without hesitation. But in metta practice, we are all one family, the family of all beings. We are all equal. We all experience suffering and we all experience joy.

Remember that the entire universe is your mind. Family, village, and country are concepts in your mind. When the mind is filled with metta, all concepts disappear. Only the feeling of metta remains. Just as the universe is endless, this practice is boundless, all-encompassing. You cannot say, "I have a small degree of metta for small beings and a big dose of metta for elephants and whales. I have low-grade metta for my adversaries and high-quality metta for my friends and family." Love does not recognize these kinds of differences. In metta, all qualities and quantities are alike.

Metta can permeate above, below, and all around. Let every tiny little space in the universe be filled with metta, so there is nowhere unaffected by this sublime state of peace. When you practice, there is nothing between you and the far corners of the universe, nothing between you and others. Metta fills the entire cosmos and spreads everywhere, without exception.

Let your loving-friendliness penetrate your own heart and the hearts of all beings.

CHAPTER 3

Eight Ways to Cultivate Loving-Friendliness

*I*n the Numerical Discourses of the Buddha (Anguttara Nikaya), the Buddha lists eight ways to cultivate loving-friendliness. He also says, "Monks, when liberating the mind through the practice of loving-friendliness has been pursued, developed, cultivated, made a vehicle and a basis, carried out, consolidated, and properly undertaken, eleven benefits are to be expected." These eight steps are progressive; they build on one another. We will discuss the eleven benefits in chapter 6.

1. "Associating" through Repetition

When we associate our minds with loving thoughts, we experience profound benefits. Affirm loving-friendliness in your thoughts and deeds, not as a chore, but in a way you truly enjoy. It will become like second nature, and resentments and fears will slowly disappear.

You can practice alone or with a group. If you are alone, speak or chant in a quiet voice. I recommend reciting the Buddha's *Discourse on Loving-Friendliness*. Appendix 2 provides "scripts" for four meditations. Because of the powerful, healing effect of the *Discourse on Loving-Friendliness*, in many Asian countries we recite it at births, weddings, housewarmings, mealtimes, morning and evening chanting, when someone is sick, and a host of other times.

Repeat loving thoughts over and over until metta takes hold in your mind. When you practice regularly and a difficult situation arises, metta will be there to help.

2. Cultivation

In order to cultivate a plant, you prepare the ground by removing weeds, rocks, and roots. You fertilize the soil, then plant seeds or bulbs. After that, you care for the tender plants until they blossom or bear fruit.

Similarly, cultivate your mind to grow loving-friendliness. This includes beginning to remove the obstacles that prevent it from blossoming—this is the practice of mindfulness meditation, which includes the practice of desisting from fueling the poisons of greed, anger, and delusion. I talk about this practice in detail in *Mindfulness in Plain English* and *Eight Mindful Steps to Happiness*. And this includes cultivation through repeating the phrases and intentions of metta—which engenders the habit of loving-friendliness, making it easier to bring loving-friendliness into your life. Practice makes it strong.

Mindfulness is one of the most important teachings of the Buddha. From the day he attained enlightenment until he passed away at the age of eighty, in almost every teaching the Buddha emphasized mindfulness. Reading in the *Discourse on Loving-Friendliness* that the Buddha considered the practice of metta as equal to that of mindfulness, we recognize how highly he regarded it. Mindfulness is essential: mindfulness discovers and sustains loving-friendliness. But mindfulness by itself is not enough. Without loving-friendliness, our practice of mindfulness will never successfully break through our contracted sense of self. Yet mindfulness is a necessary basis for developing loving-friendliness. The two are always developed together.

Thoughts of loving-friendliness prevent greed, hatred, and delu-

sion from overtaking us. We pray that all beings will live in peace
and harmony.

3. Amplification

Olympic athletes practice arduously, sometimes beginning in childhood. We must practice loving-friendliness with the same focused
dedication. The more we practice, the more consistently peace will
prevail in our minds. Just as we feed our bodies the best-quality food
available, we can nourish our minds with metta. And the more we
practice loving-friendliness, the more skilled we become at sending
it outward to the whole universe and all living beings, the more its
power and effect grow, become amplified.

As your loving-friendliness grows it becomes more stable; you
may find that even when somebody is very upset with you, you can
still maintain your composure. You can remain calm and cool if you
are practicing metta. When your mind is fully charged with loving-
friendliness you can help an angry person calmly and peacefully. You
can see how the other person suffers from his or her anger. When
your response is calm and relaxed the other person also can become
calm soon. This comes to you naturally.

4. Vehicle

The Pali word for vehicle, *yana*, is used to describe ways of practice
or schools of study. If we carry forth this imagery that the Buddha
used, see metta as your mode of transport, as your vehicle for
encountering your life and all beings. In the *Discourse on Two Kinds
of Thought* (*Dvedhavitakka Sutta*), the Buddha points out that whatever we repeat in our mind becomes a habit. When metta reaches
the point of becoming a habit or a reflex, we can rely on it to bring
us peace and happiness. Whether standing, sitting, walking, speaking, or engaged in work, in every waking moment our mind becomes
filled with loving-friendliness. We no longer need to make an effort

to cultivate it. It's simply present, always—a pervasive, wholesome habit that prevents us from becoming defensive or reactive.

This vehicle takes you on the divine path to liberate the mind from anger, greed, and delusion. Based on this vehicle you can practice all the factors of enlightenment.

5. *Ground*

Make metta practice the ground for growing happiness and cultivating concentration. Make metta a basis for wholesome thoughts, words, and deeds. Let metta be the foundation of generosity, morality, and sharing. Let it become the very ground on which you stand. The ground represents steadiness. When our metta practice is steady we experience steady peace and happiness, the kind that is not dissolved by mere circumstance. We can gain meditative concentration easily by standing on this steady ground.

6. *Experience*

Metta is not a philosophy or a theory. It is an experience, based on practice. Through consistent and sustained practice, it becomes your own direct experience. Bring loving-friendliness into your daily life; experience it in your heart and mind. This is of utmost importance. Whatever comes from your heart affects people deeply.

The Buddha spoke from his heart, and he opened people's wisdom door. He taught that we must establish ourselves in the practice first before advising others. Only when our practice is grounded in experience will it be able to help others.

Therefore, as you begin in your practice of loving-friendliness, practice without expecting recognition. You don't need people to know that you practice metta. Do it quietly. When you live with this attitude, you are practicing metta. You *are* loving-friendliness. Remember, practice makes perfect!

7. *Habit*

Reflecting on loving-friendliness helps us feel calm, peaceful, and happy. If we contemplate something once, we get a taste, but it isn't enough to make it a habit. To make metta an automatic response like breathing or blinking, put the fruit of your meditation into action, whether someone sees you doing it or not, whether anyone appreciates you for doing it or not. As one famous saying goes, "Sow an act, and you reap a habit. Sow a habit, and you reap a character. Sow a character, and you reap a destiny." This is the power of habit.

8. *Practicing Well*

Greed and hatred are the roots of all suffering. We practice metta to overcome suffering. We must practice well to fully reach this place.

How do we practice well? Start the day with loving thoughts. As soon as you wake up in the morning, remember that you want to live a healthy and peaceful life. What you do early in the morning has an impact on your mind the rest of the day. Be friendly with yourself, be warm. Be loving and kind. Don't cause yourself harm in thought, word, or deed. Forgive those who have offended you. Don't put yourself in a higher position than others. Understand that we all have weaknesses. All of this opens the door to truly understanding the roots suffering. And when we truly understand suffering, we can truly practice well throughout each day and throughout our life.

All eight steps of practice must be lived, enacted—practiced mentally, verbally, *and* physically every day, not just while sitting in meditation or reciting the *Metta Sutta*.

When metta is infused in your actions, the eight steps of practice are present in each moment.

Your life goes more smoothly and honestly, and others will feel it.

CHAPTER 4

Practicing Peace

*P*racticing loving-friendliness is a gentle way to attain happiness and to *be* peace.

Visualize the world of loving-friendliness you aspire to be part of. See its contours, within and without. Bear it in mind as you cultivate loving-friendliness while reciting the *Metta Sutta* and when being honest and friendly in daily life. When you are honest, you trust others because you trust yourself. Trusting yourself means you know yourself, including aspects you might be ashamed of—and this requires honestly looking at yourself, and aspiring to live from loving-friendliness. It may seem paradoxical, but knowing your own vulnerability, unreliability, and weakness gives a sense of security, and that makes your mind peaceful. Don't stop trying to act in ways the wise ones would approve, but take into account your strengths and weaknesses as you do so. Others cannot give you peace. Tell the truth, and so be free.

We all have difficulties and need to support one another. When we practice loving-friendliness in a transparent way, we can attain the highest peace. This is not like a negotiated peace between countries. It is spiritual peace in our own heart. Metta can be an integral part of a happy life. Metta brings harmony to ourselves and society. It cannot be separated from life or practiced only in seclusion.

Metta is not an esoteric practice. There is no secret to it. The qualities of loving-friendliness are always within us, hidden in our subconscious mind under layers of greed, hatred, and delusion. We need to clear away the brush to give the flowers a chance to grow. Most flowers grow in soft, fertile soil, not in dry, stone-like land. Loving-friendliness is just such fertile soil in our lives.

Loving-friendliness is, ultimately, natural—a part of our being. Children are relaxed and make friends easily. Adults can be so stiff. You can be friendly without being naive. Try initiating a conversation by saying good morning, good evening, or good afternoon to a stranger—really be honest in this simple expression, really care. Be willing to take a chance on loving-friendliness, regardless of how others might react. Metta practitioners can speak first and even smile.

It is important to be sincere in your metta practice. Notice your mind as you say, "May I be well, happy, and peaceful. May my parents, teachers, relatives, friends, unknown persons, hostile persons, and all beings be well, happy, and peaceful." Or when you tell others good morning, good afternoon, or good evening. If you are living from your heart, if you explore the world and yourself with candor, even if the other person doesn't respond, you still feel peace and wish them well.

I remember watching the *CBS Evening News* when I was in Washington, DC. Dan Rather showed a clip of an old man standing in front of his house by the Washington beltway, waving to people who were driving to work in the morning. "Good morning. Have a good day!" In the evening, he would say, "Good evening. Have a safe drive home!" Dan Rather asked him, "Sir, why do you do this? No one can see or hear you. Aren't you wasting your time?" He said, "No, Mr. Rather. I know they can't see me or hear me. I just wish them a good morning, a good evening, and a safe drive. I do it from my heart; I mean what I say."

Several years later, the old man passed away, and Dan Rather announced it on the news. This man did what he did with a pure heart, without expecting reward or recognition. He didn't even care if people saw or heard him doing it. The depth of his metta touched my heart.

Practicing metta is a way to care for our own wounds. If others respond negatively, they might be going through something; we don't know. When we feel hostility or anger, it's a thorn in our own heart. We can remove it by practicing loving-friendliness, sharing our love. Doing so expresses the uprightness of a disciple of the Buddha.

We should be upright, not uptight. We can learn to love ourselves, both our gifts and our demons, without hesitation. Don't think you don't deserve love. If you don't love yourself, who will? Caring for yourself in this way is not selfishness. Take care of your body and mind without abusing yourself with alcohol, harmful drugs, careless eating, mindless behavior, smoking, and not getting enough rest. Be friendly with yourself before you try to share friendliness with others. Telling lies, for example, hurts you more than it hurts others. Killing, stealing, and sensual misconduct hurt you. If you love yourself, avoid harmful actions.

This is the straight path to liberation, built by honesty, focus, and wisdom. Freedom from fear is not denial. Freedom from anger is not suppression. Metta directs us to follow the Buddha's direct path, which is the path of truth. No one else can know what is in our heart, how metta pervades our body and mind.

Saturate every cell of your being with metta and it will naturally radiate forth.

You can't pretend. This practice must be done honestly.

And always begin with yourself.

Tell yourself honestly, "As I want to have a healthy mind and a healthy body, I must understand how anger arises. I must be friends with myself and experience peace. Through destructive habits of mind and body, I've suffered in the past. Unhealthy habits harm me. I need to see them clearly and practice metta toward myself." Then follow the truth that metta practice reveals.

If you are bossy, pushy, or crude, expressing resentment through your thoughts, words, and deeds, you distance yourself from others. A metta practitioner can be gentle—a gentleman or a lady. Don't be arrogant. Act humbly, without conceit. If someone points out your mistakes, don't criticize them back, saying, "Mind your own business. Do you know how many offenses you've committed?" If we think highly of ourselves and look down on others, metta practice will be difficult. Metta equalizes us all; we're all equal on life's journey. We each have our own karma. Instead, think, "I have enough suffering to make me humble. There is no basis for pride or arrogance. We're all in the same boat after all."

Practice metta for the benefit of all beings. Be humble and pay attention to others. There is nothing to lose. Your meditation room is not a battlefield. You are just trying to find peace and live in harmony. There is no basis for conceit, no basis for struggle. We are all subject to illness, old age, and death. We must leave everything behind. Even if we exercise, eat well, meditate, and take good care of our body, we'll still die one day and leave our health and wealth behind. Our karma is our only true possession. If we live and die with metta, our mind will be at peace.

CHAPTER 5

Metta in Action

In May 1975, a month after the Vietnam War ended, the US State Department called to ask if I would serve as Buddhist chaplain at a refugee camp in Florida. Vietnamese fleeing their country were arriving in great numbers there. I'd had no experience working with refugees and did not speak Vietnamese or French, but I said yes. Then I called a friend, John Garges, who had worked with refugees and spoke some French, and he agreed to accompany me.

Two days later, we were the only two passengers on a military jet to Eglin Air Force Base near Pensacola, Florida. We were given a comfortable bungalow, and my duties were explained. I was to console ten thousand Vietnamese who were arriving, perform religious services, and provide whatever other spiritual comfort I could. There were also Catholic and Protestant clergymen at the camp to serve refugees who had converted to those faiths.

Just two hours after we arrived, John and I greeted a planeload of refugees wearing ragged clothes, carrying little or nothing. They seemed in shock, and many were crying, especially the children. Some were obviously sick or wounded; others appeared to be emotionally disturbed. Some clung to the hands of strangers. Too many had been separated from their loved ones. When they saw me in orange robes, many of them smiled. Others burst into tears and bowed to me over and over. Every day we met planeloads of refugees, and the scene repeated itself. The familiar sight of a Buddhist monk seemed to be a life preserver for many of the Vietnamese, who were scarred by war and now transported to an alien land.

My work with the refugees was very rewarding. I felt I was providing comfort to people at a very difficult time in their lives. That was the easy part. The hard part was getting along with some of the other clergymen. Some considered this an opportunity to evangelize; after all, there were thousands of souls right there to save.

Religious services were held under a large tent, and the different denominations took turns leading them. When I held services, I put a Buddha statue on the altar. When the Catholics or Protestants held their services, they put a cross on the altar. The tent for services was next to a smaller tent where I had my office. One day, while I was working, I saw about thirty children being herded into the large tent. Many looked no older than ten. One of the Protestant ministers, a particularly zealous man, was with them. I heard him start intoning the rites of baptism, and I hurried over and interrupted the ceremony.

"Joseph, what you're doing is wrong," I said. "I've seen you going all over the camp, talking to these kids' parents, trying to convert them." We both knew most of the children would end up Christian. Every one of the religious organizations sponsoring the refugees was Christian. They would be resettled and compelled to go to Christian churches. But that would come later. I thought it was wrong to start converting them before they'd even left the camp.

"These refugees are like drowning people," I told him. "They'll grasp onto anything you tell them, because they're desperate to get out of this camp. Have you seen me trying to convert any of the Christian refugees back to Buddhism?"

I was livid. I went straight to the State Department's office on base and reported what was happening. I told the officer that these kinds of conversions would give the entire operation a bad name. The next day in the refugee camp newsletter, there was an article giving strict orders not to convert anyone in the camp to another religion.

Thankfully, most of the other clergy were tolerant of one another. One day, I was talking to two Catholic priests, one Vietnamese and one American. The American priest had two rosaries hanging around his neck, one with a cross on it and the other with a small Buddha figure. He said that that morning they had gotten so intertwined, he could hardly untangle them. "That shows that the Buddha and the cross should never be mixed," said the Vietnamese priest.

"No, no," I said. "It shows that the Buddha and Jesus love each other so much that you can't separate them." For me, this was an expression of the loving-friendliness in my heart, of how I saw the world.

Another part of my job was to help locate sponsors—families or individuals who would agree to take a few refugees into their community and help them find housing and jobs. One woman who had agreed to sponsor a young Vietnamese man brought him back to the camp saying she wanted to "return" him. She had taken care of him for a month. "I thought he was a good Christian," she said, her mouth set in a frown.

"He's not a good Christian?" I asked.

"Not at all," she said, obviously disappointed.

"What is his religion?"

"He's Buddhist," she snapped. "I just found out."

"And what made you think he was a Christian?" I asked.

"Because he's kind and polite. He's very patient and he always treats me respectfully." I often ran up against that kind of discrimination.

Not long after my arrival at the base, a strongly worded editorial appeared in the local newspaper. How could the US government use taxpayers' money to bring a pagan to help the poor Vietnamese refugees at the camp? If those miserable people don't become Christians, the writer declared, then let them go to hell. Just don't use our tax dollars to teach a satanic religion.

In my life now, my response to discrimination is usually loving-friendliness, a pure, unadulterated desire for the well-being of others, a love without attachment or expectation, practiced unconditionally. It's the ultimate underlying principle behind all wholesome thoughts, words, and deeds. Metta transcends barriers of religion, culture, geography, language, and nationality. Loving-friendliness is the reliable path to peace, to warm connection. It is a universal and ancient law that binds all of us together. We need it in order to live and work together harmoniously. Especially because of our differences, we need loving-friendliness. And when we extend metta toward others, our own lives become happier and more peaceful. I used the power of metta every day in that refugee camp. The refugees needed it to help heal their psychological and emotional wounds. I needed it, too, to stay strong enough to work with them in such painful circumstances. And those who opposed what I was doing—well, quite frankly, they needed it, too.

CHAPTER 6

Benefits of Loving-Friendliness

We don't need an ideal society or a perfect world to practice loving-friendliness. We aren't practicing to save the world or make it perfect. We practice for ourselves, for our own peace and well-being. Any effects beyond that are byproducts. If the focus is outside ourselves, we will never succeed. But fortunately, our own well-being is intimately bound up with the well-being of others; so truly practicing loving-friendliness for our own benefit does benefit others.

In the *Discourse on the Benefits of Loving-Friendliness (Metta Nisamsa Sutta)*, the Buddha lists eleven benefits derived from practicing metta—and I might add that many of these benefits are being confirmed by contemporary scientific research!

Here is the Buddha's list:

1. You sleep well.
When you go to bed feeling loving-friendliness toward yourself and others, you will be relaxed and will sleep peacefully.

2. You wake up feeling well.
When you get a good night's sleep, you wake up feeling rested and relaxed. With a relaxed mind and body, you are able to connect with family, friends, relatives, neighbors, and even strangers in a genuine and centered way. You feel fresh, uplifted, and joyful all day.

3. You're not likely to have nightmares.

When you practice metta, you become solid enough to face whatever arises. And in fact, the Buddha said it's unlikely you'll have nightmares when you practice metta.

4. Your body relaxes and your face is joyful.

Your body reflects your mind. When you feel love for all beings, it shows on your face. Seeing your honest, relaxed face, others will gravitate toward you and enjoy being around you.

5. Even animals and celestial beings feel drawn to you.

When you practice metta, your mind generates a peaceful field around you. Children especially are tuned in to this energy—and non-humans feel it too!

One day I was walking my dog, Brown, and a couple came toward us. The woman kneeled down to Brown's level and talked to him. He wagged his tail and became affectionate with her. The man was frightened, and Brown growled at him.

6. Spirits protect you.

There are times we feel guided and protected by beings beyond our sight. Recognizing this as a kind of grace is a source of serenity. Whether it's literally true or there is some other energy that gives us this sense of guidance and protection, the Buddha included this among the benefits of practicing metta. Remember the response of the forest spirits when the monks began reciting the *Metta Sutta*.

7. Fire, poisons, and weapons will not harm you.

When we read stories of old, many of the elements are symbolic or mythic. The Buddha shared tales of adepts who practiced metta and were protected from fire, poisons, and weapons. He explained that greed, hatred, and delusion are the fires, the poisons, and the weapons against which metta protects us.

In the *Fire Sermon* (*Aditta Pariyaya Sutta*), the Buddha said that poison is of three kinds—greed, hatred, and delusion. These weapons, like daggers, he said, can cut your peace into pieces. In the Numerical Discourses of the Buddha, the Buddha described bodily, verbal, and mental weapons. In the Udana, he said, "They quarrel, squabble, and argue with each other, stabbing each other with verbal daggers: 'This is Dharma. That is not.'" In the Dhammapada, the Buddha said, "There is no fire like greed, no misfortune like hatred, no suffering like delusion, and no greater happiness than peace."

In a well-known story about the power of metta, Uttara, a devoted follower of the Buddha, was bereft. She had been given in marriage to a man who did not have high regard for the Buddha, and so she hadn't seen the Buddha or his disciples for two and a half months. She was feeling forlorn, and her father suggested she hire a courtesan to serve her husband while she joined the Buddha and his community for the final two weeks of their rainy-season retreat. Uttara agreed and was able to serve the Buddha and his disciples as a cook and attend his teachings.

One day as he was looking out the window of his mansion, Uttara's husband saw her working in the retreat kitchen wearing a stained apron and thought it pathetic she was attending the retreat rather than indulging in the luxuries of life with him. Noticing his disdain for his wife, Sirima, the courtesan, began plotting to harm Uttara so she herself could become the man's wife. Sirima boiled some ghee and left the house to splash it on Uttara.

When Uttara saw the courtesan coming to harm her, she meditated on loving-friendliness and remained completely at peace. At the same time, Uttara's maidservants also saw this foul deed unfolding and ran to stop Sirima. The maids tackled Sirima and began pummeling her, when Uttara intervened to save her attacker. After that, Uttara bathed Sirima in warm water and massaged her body with herbs and oil to soothe her wounds. Sirima fell to the ground and begged Uttara's forgiveness. Uttara said she would forgive Sirima if the Buddha advised it.

The next day, Sirima asked the Buddha to forgive what she had tried to do. The Buddha asked Uttara how she felt as Sirima was pouring boiling ghee on her, and Uttara responded, "I was grateful to Sirima for serving my husband so I could spend two weeks with the noble community. I had no ill will toward her, only loving-friendliness." The Buddha commended her, "Well done, Uttara. By not bearing ill will, you were able to conquer the one who abuses you. By being generous, you conquered the one who is stingy. By speaking the truth, you conquered one who lies." Upon the advice of the Buddha, Uttara forgave Sirima, and Sirima took refuge in the Buddha.

In another story, the Buddha told of Culasiva Thera, who was not at all affected by poison because of his profound practice of metta. A Dhammapada commentary tells of four novice monks whose practice of loving-friendliness was so profound they were unaffected by a weapon. Not only were disciples of the Buddha protected by metta, but in one story *a cow* was spared being shot with an arrow because of her love and affection nursing her calf.

The Buddha taught that the six senses—seeing, hearing, smelling, tasting, touching, and cognizing—are on fire. Any one of them is sufficient to consume us. The antidote, he taught, is to know reality. Be mindful and see how sensations and states affect you. Think of your own experience; see how much you burn with the fire of greed, hatred, and delusion, and how much you poison your mind with greed, hatred, and delusion. When you practice metta, your breathing becomes calm and you feel so much love and compassion that your mind naturally wishes all beings to live in peace and harmony.

8. *Your mind immediately becomes calm.*

Metta stimulates a friendly feeling that makes us calm and happy. It truly is a wonderful way of life!

9. *Your complexion brightens.*

Metta shows in your face. As you practice metta, joy arises. At first it is barely noticeable, but as the joy increases, it begins to pervade your whole mind and body. Metta does not rely on any particular time, place, or condition. Once aroused, it can remain present in you the rest of your life. Your face cannot hide what is going on in your mind. When you are angry, it shows on your face. When you are peaceful, everyone notices. The energy of metta spreads through your bloodstream and nourishes your whole being. You look bright and clear, calm and peaceful.

10. *You'll die with a clear mind.*

The thought of dying peacefully can be comforting. When we have unresolved conflicts, death can be difficult. Loving-friendliness can make dying easier for the one passing away and for those around her.

There is a difference between true peace and the appearance of peace. You may seem cheerful; you might even make people laugh. But when you are approaching death, if greed, hatred, and delusion are still lurking deep down in your psyche, that joviality will vanish. Practicing loving-friendliness sinks into the depths of your consciousness and makes your mind genuinely calm. With metta, you will die peacefully, without confusion.

In the Anguttara Nikaya, Samavati, the wife of the king the Buddha had declared chief among those who practiced metta, was burned alive while leading a loving-friendliness retreat for women. Magandiya was the culprit. So proud of her rare beauty, Magandiya rejected suitor after suitor. One day her father saw the

Buddha sitting under a tree and asked him to marry his daughter. The Buddha explained his vow of celibacy and declined in a way that Magandiya found offensive, and she was determined to seek revenge. Magandiya knew that Samavati was one of the Buddha's favorite laywomen, so she set fire to the house where Samavati was leading a metta retreat for five hundred women. They all died in the fire.

As she lay dying, Samavati declared, "Over many lifetimes our bodies have been burned over and over again. As you pass from birth to death and back to birth, be heedful!" Her words were so powerful that the five hundred women dying alongside her were inspired to practice metta meditation in their final moments. Although their bodies were burned by fire, their minds were free.

11. You'll die in peace.

If at the time of death you do not yet comprehend the highest truth, you will still go to a realm of great peace.

If you have not completed the path of awakening before you die, the peaceful mental state generated by metta will still allow you to be reborn in a heavenly realm.

Regardless of whether we consider heaven a real or figurative place, this portends well and encourages us to practice loving-friendliness while we can.

CHAPTER 7

A Mother's Love

The Buddha encouraged us to cultivate the four noble states of being, which in Pali are known as the *brahmaviharas*. *Brahma* means "noble" or "divine," referring to spirits who dwell in higher realms of consciousness. *Vihara* means "abode" or "refuge." The brahmaviharas—loving-friendliness, compassion, appreciative or sympathetic joy, and equanimity—encourage us to bring forth our best qualities. These four states are interrelated; we cannot develop one without the other. One way to understand this is to think of different stages of parenthood. A good mother has all four noble states of being in her.

When a woman becomes pregnant, she feels a tremendous outpouring of love for the child inside her womb. She'll do everything she can to ensure the baby's well-being. She radiates loving, hopeful thoughts for the child. Like metta, the feeling an expectant mother has for her child is limitless and all-embracing, not contingent upon specific behaviors.

After the baby is born and begins exploring the world, his parents develop compassion. Every time he scrapes his knee, falls down, or bumps his head, his mom and dad feel his pain. Some parents say that when their child feels pain, it's as though they themselves have been hurt. There is no pity in this feeling. Pity puts a distance between you and others. Compassion leads to appropriate action from a place of connection, and the appropriate action is the pure, heartfelt hope that the pain will subside and the child will feel better.

As time passes, the child heads off to school. The parents watch the youngster make friends and enter into studies, sports, and other activities. Maybe the child does well on a spelling test, makes the baseball team, or gets elected class president. The parents are naturally not jealous or resentful of their child's success, but are filled with happiness for him. This is appreciative or sympathetic joy. Think about how you might feel for your own child. You can feel this for others. Even when you think of others whose success exceeds your own, you can cultivate the capacity to appreciate their achievement and rejoice in their happiness just as a mother naturally does for her child.

Seeing the success of others, we can be happy for them without becoming jealous. Think of a good friend who is currently successful. Visualize her laughing and relaxed. If your friend is not successful now, you still can be happy for her, thinking of her past successes. If she was not successful in the past and is not successful now, she might be successful in the future due to her capacities and skills. Seeing her working very hard to be successful in the future, you can be happy for her.

Now visualize someone about whom your feeling is neutral who is successful in many ways. Seeing or hearing of her success, although you hardly know her, conjure up the feeling of happiness for her.

Now envision someone who is your adversary. If he is successful in overcoming his negative mental state now, or he has been successful in the past, or is going to be successful in the future, you can be happy for him too.

Finally, appreciate your own successes, past, present, and future. In this practice, you start with those close to you, then neutral persons, then adversaries, putting yourself as the last person toward whom you direct appreciative joy.

Returning to the mother and her child—eventually, after many years, the child grows up. He finishes school and goes out on his own. Perhaps the child marries and starts a family. Now it is time for the parents to practice equanimity. Clearly what the parents feel for the child is not indifference. It is an appreciation that they have done all they could for him. They recognize their limitations. Of course the parents continue to care for and respect their child, but they do so with awareness that they no longer steer the outcome of his life. This is the practice of equanimity.

Just as with loving-friendliness, practice extending equanimity to all sorts of people. Practice equanimity with a neutral person, then a dear person, then a hostile person, and finally oneself.

Equanimity is peaceful and sublime. Once you have mastered true equanimity, you can bring it to mind at will. In the *Discourse That Takes Place in the Town of Devadaha (Devadaha Sutta)*, the Buddha advised meditators to develop equanimity, explaining that we experience distress according to the extent to which we identify with external circumstances, and not according to the circumstances themselves. Equanimity can be cultivated in the same way as metta and made boundless, spreading to the six directions.

The Buddha described "equanimity that is based on diversity," meaning equanimity developed on sights, sounds, smells, flavors, tangible objects, and thoughts. Imagine trying to fulfill your desire for a particular object, when you realize that the depth of the feeling is in you, not the object. Realizing this, you can loosen the bonds of attachment and not identify with a particular outcome. That is the equanimity of diversity.

On the other hand, the equanimity developed through concentration on one object is called "equanimity of unity." Additionally, equanimity maintained from the base of infinite space, and through to the base of neither-perception-nor-nonperception, also belongs to the category of equanimity of unity.

During meditation, we may see that everything belonging to past, present, and future is impermanent, not ultimately or lastingly satisfying, and without a fixed essential nature. This is known as "equanimity of renunciation."

We develop these four sublime states—loving-friendliness, compassion, appreciative joy, and equanimity—as we face challenges in life. There are ample opportunities to practice all four sublime states. We put them to use as situations arise. We don't have to employ them all at once or for just one person. As we grow in mindfulness, we will know when and where to use these sublime states. The Buddha teaches that if we practice loving-friendliness, compassion, appreciative joy, and equanimity with clear comprehension and mindfulness from childhood until old age, our minds will be liberated from greed, hatred, and delusion.

Metta is present in all four noble states. When we practice metta, then compassion, appreciative joy, and equanimity grow naturally in our minds. You will naturally be compassionate when loving-friendliness grows in your heart. You will not be jealous of others' success; covetousness—craving for someone else's property—does not arise in a heart full of metta. Rather you wish the whole world to be prosperous and peaceful.

In late 1976, I got a letter from my younger sister saying our mother wasn't well, and that she hardly ate anymore. Tucked into the letter was a note from my mother. It was only a few lines, but at the end of it she said that it had taken her a week to write it. She was so weak she couldn't write more than one or two letters at a time. It was hard even to hold the pen. But she was determined to write me herself. She probably knew it was going to be her last letter to me. "I wish I could see you," she wrote.

"You should come home," said the letter from my sister. "She may not live much longer." With permission of the board of the Washington Buddhist Vihara, where I lived and taught, I boarded a Pan Am 747 and headed home to Sri Lanka.

On the way, I had a stopover in Malaysia. Some friends there donated a slide projector to me. I had about five hundred color slides of places I'd visited all over the world—there were temples, skyscrapers, landscapes, animals, and festivals. I wanted to show my mother where I had been all these years while I was gone from home.

When I arrived in Sri Lanka, we had the slide show at my sister's house. Because there was no electricity there, we had to run extension cords from her neighbor's house. My mother sat, fascinated, as she looked at the slides and listened to my narration. Her eyes were shining.

We started the show at ten o'clock at night, and it went on until two o'clock in the morning, and my mother never seemed to get tired. When it was over, she asked if there were any more slides. That was our last good time together. She died en route to a hospital in Kandy just one day later. Mother insisted on sitting up in the backseat, instead of lying down. By the time they got to the hospital, she was silent. She had died in the backseat of the car, sitting upright. If an ambulance were available to transport her to the hospital she would likely have lived for a few more months.

I thought about how many times my mother had nursed my wounds when I was a child, how she always knew exactly what to do to make me feel better. I remembered how her arms felt, wrapped around me. I thought of that last letter she had written me so painstakingly, just a few lines—four lines, to be exact. I was so sorry she had died in pain and regretted that I hadn't been with her. My mother was a walking example of metta, treating everyone she met with gentleness and soft words. In many ways, I considered her almost a holy person.

"To be separated from loved ones is suffering," the Buddha said. Although I had spent years delivering sermons about grief and sorrow, conducting funerals, and consoling people after the death of relatives, I didn't really understand those words of the Buddha until I experienced the loss of my mother. When she died, my grief was so intense that my heart felt as though it had been injected with some bitter, painful substance.

All through my monastic career up to that point, I realized that on some level I was always striving to please my mother. I wanted to make her happy, more than any other person in the world. She was so proud that I was a monk and that I was teaching Dharma all over the globe. So every time I achieved something new or did something worthwhile, I wrote her a letter about it, not to boast but because I knew how much pleasure it would bring her. Now that she was gone—who would I try to please?

My attachment to my mother was the strongest fetter I had. When I lost her, I temporarily forgot all of the Buddha's teachings about death and impermanence. I was simply awash in sorrow. Even today, I feel great fondness for the memory of my mother. In 1979 or 1980, I was speaking at an interfaith conference in Dallas. Because it was near Thanksgiving, we were asked to speak about gratitude. I decided to speak about my mother. But when I stood at the podium and tried to say the first words of my speech, I started crying. It was embarrassing. I was sobbing so hard I couldn't speak at all. The audience just sat, watching me. It took me a long time to gain my composure.

All I wanted to say to them was that I would never forget my mother, and that I was grateful for her endless love. Instead, standing there crying before that auditorium full of people, I came to understand one of the Buddha's statements about death and grieving. He said the tears we have shed over the death of our mothers in all our past lives—those tears are greater than all the water in all the oceans.

A mother's love for her child is immeasurable. She would do anything for her child. She would even sacrifice her own life to protect her child. While going through extreme suffering, some mothers live for the sake of their child. Consider what it might be like to live with this kind of loving-friendliness for all beings.

Loving-friendliness is a principle we want to uphold all the time. We saw in the stories of Samavati and Uttara how they never stopped cultivating metta. Samavati, while dying, protected her metta and asked her companions to do the same, even though they too were losing their lives. Uttara would have become disfigured when Sirima poured boiling ghee on her body, yet she rescued her perpetrator from being attacked by her housemaids and forgave her. She even brought her to the Buddha's teachings. They did not lose their metta even in those very difficult situations. We too can preserve our metta, just like we uphold the principles of honesty, respect, and dignity. The only practical way to practice this instruction of the Buddha is to protect our own thoughts of loving-friendliness, compassion, appreciative joy, and equanimity. As a passage in the *Path of Purification* (*Visuddhimagga*) states:

> As a hen guards her eggs,
> Or as a yak her tail,
> Or like a darling child,
> Or like an only eye—

So you who are engaged
Your virtue to protect,
Be prudent at all times
And ever scrupulous.

When we sincerely wish all living beings to be well, happy, and peaceful, then we are well, happy, and peaceful.

The Buddha taught that we can cultivate boundless metta. Our metta is not limited by time or place; it extends to infinity and eternity. This does not mean we must go around the world physically protecting every living being. That would be impossible. It means we should protect our own metta, just as a mother protects her only child.

The Buddha teaches in the *Metta Sutta*:

Even as a mother protects with her life
    Her child, her only child,
So with a boundless heart
    Should one cherish all beings;
Radiating kindness over the entire world:
    Spreading upward to the skies,
And downward to the depths;
    Outward and unbounded,
Freed from hatred and ill will.

Your metta is your child. Protect it just as a loving mother would protect her only child.

When obstacles arise, don't give up. Keep your good heart open!

CHAPTER 8

Overcoming Ill Will

*A*s a practice that trains the mind to become gentle and considerate, metta is a powerful method to dissolve our habits of thinking about, speaking to, and treating others with ill will.

In the *Discourse on Repression of Ill Will* (*Aghata Vinaya Sutta*), Sariputta, one of the Buddha's leading disciples, offers five practices for overcoming ill will and practicing loving-friendliness. These examples show us simple ways to think about complex, difficult situations. When we are with others, as our metta is sprouting in our hearts, we may face situations that challenge us. We know that we need to overcome whatever ill will remains in our minds toward others, but we are tempted to fall into old patterns of judging and distancing ourselves from them. These practices offer a different way of interacting with people who anger us.

The Dirty Rag

We may come across people whose words are kind, but whose bodily behavior is not. They make promises they can't keep and act evasively, or say nice things to us but act poorly. We can consider behaving toward them like the monk who, while walking down the road, comes across a dirty rag. The rag is so filthy he can't even pick it up with his hands, so he holds it with one foot while he kicks it with the other foot to clean it off. Then he picks it up with two fingers, shakes it off, brings it home, and washes it. He sees that this once-dirty rag is in fact completely functional, and he sews it onto his patchwork robes!

When we encounter people whose deeds are not good but whose words are pleasant, we can search for ways to arouse loving-friendliness within ourselves. We can certainly find one reason or another to do so—we can grasp onto their kind words in the same way the monk saw the value of the cloth obscured by dirt. We admire and respect these people for their words and arouse our own loving-friendliness to share with them. If we are able to associate with them and show them loving-friendliness, it might encourage them to change their way of acting. But we do not pay attention to their actions. Focusing on and encouraging others' positive words gives their kindness room to blossom naturally. Additionally, when we learn to practice compassion and equanimity toward people in this way, our own thoughts of ill will toward them are subdued.

Keep in mind that the layers of conditioning on a person have made them difficult to handle just like the layers of dirt on the cloth. Perhaps they have faced hardship unknown to us—such as losing a friend or family member, home, or job. Maybe they were mistreated or abused as a child and this contributed to their thinking rough behavior is a normal part of life. What matters for us is that we see that someone is suffering. We can offer them our loving-friendliness.

The Algae-Covered Pond

Next, consider how you become angry with a person whose speech is unkind but whose actions are respectful. For example, someone disparages you for doing a task incorrectly but then does the task for you so that you can learn from them. Sariputta compares this type of person to a pond covered with algae. Say that there is a pond nearby on a hot day when you are very thirsty. You are sweaty and feeling exhausted, and a cool dip would feel so refreshing. But the pond is covered with algae, so how do you dive in? First you must clear the algae away with both hands.

Similarly, you can overlook this person's challenges and recognize that their heart opens to compassion and loving-friendliness from time to time. On this basis, you develop loving-friendliness toward that person. The ill will you may have felt toward them diminishes on its own.

The Hoof-Print Puddle

The third type of person speaks both unwholesome words and does unwholesome deeds, but from time to time their heart opens to noble, friendly, and compassionate things. Sariputta suggests such a person can be compared to a puddle on the road.

Suppose you are walking along a road and there is no water or well. You are thirsty and tired, desperately looking for water. Almost dehydrated, you find a little rainwater that has collected in the hoof print of a cow in the middle of the road. There's very little water, and if you try to scoop it up by hand, you'll make it muddy. What to do? You kneel down and slowly bring your mouth to that bit of water and sip it without disturbing the mud, thus quenching your thirst.

From time to time, even with their bad words and deeds, you'll find that this person's heart opens to loving-friendliness, compassion, appreciative joy, and equanimity. When you recognize a moment when their heart is open, take advantage of it—enter quickly. Say some loving words to keep their heart open. Speak kindly, showing metta in your tone and words. This is a wonderful opportunity to share with someone the benefit of metta. By patiently practicing loving-friendliness toward this person, despite all their weaknesses, you can produce a miracle. Others might give up and over time get tired and burn out. They might blame metta, saying it doesn't work;

while it is a normal reaction to blame something that doesn't work, look closely. If you do something haphazardly and fail, don't blame the system. Find out what could be done differently and make the necessary adjustments.

Similarly, you can find a way even with this kind of person to cultivate loving-friendliness. Use whatever possible opening you can get to overcome your feelings of ill will, just as you would sip the water in the cow's hoof print.

The Sick Traveler

The fourth type of person you may feel ill will toward has no visible redeeming qualities: their words are negative, their behavior is bad, and their heart does not open at all for anything noble.

Coming across such a person is like finding a patient, a sick man, walking alone on a road where there is no hospital, no village, and no other humans around. There is no water, no house to rest in, not a single tree to provide him shelter. This person is afflicted and suffering from severe sickness. He needs immediate medical attention—otherwise he will die. You see him and feel very sorry for him. Your heart melts. You think, "How can I help this man? He needs water, medicine, food, and clothes. He needs somebody to help him." When your heart responds with empathy you find a way to help this person. Listen to that voice that wants to help him, and let that spark of kindness grow. Then you will volunteer to help that person in spite of any difficulty.

Similarly, when people are completely negative in thought, word, and deed, we can practice metta. Although we might normally react to them with anger, still we need to find a reason to develop thoughts of loving-friendliness and compassion toward them. Then we become like the sick person's medicine.

One who practices metta should think about how this person's unwholesome behavior creates so much suffering for himself, both now and in the future. If this man gives up his bad behavior and cultivates wholesome bodily and verbal behavior then he could find peace and happiness in this life. He could enjoy things available to him without grumbling. He could have many friends and live a happy and healthy life. So instead think: "I should help him to get rid of his hatred; if I do, I will be glad for the rest of my life thinking that I have done something wonderful." Rather than being angry with such a person, let your heart open to him to see how much he suffers by acting in such a harmful way.

The Clear Lake

The fifth person's words and behavior are sweet, and their heart is open for noble practices.

This person can be likened to a clear, calm lake. The water is sweet and cool, and the pool is surrounded by soft grass and shade trees. If someone comes along tired and overheated, taking a dip in this lake is most refreshing. In a similar way, this person's thoughts are sweet and wonderful, and their words are beautiful and friendly. Their deeds are friendly, beautiful, and pure. Everything is ideal. It is easy for us to cultivate loving-friendliness toward that person. If you are unable to calm the anger you may feel toward such a person, reflect on their good qualities without harboring any jealousy. Know that it is possible for you as well to become like a clear lake in your thoughts, words, and deeds.

Consider the ways in which you can try to cultivate loving-friendliness equally toward all these five types of people without discrimination. Of course, you may find that it is not very easy—that there are times when you want to give in to ill will. Stretching our capacity for loving-friendliness sometimes requires that we make a great sacrifice—but what we sacrifice are our comfort, thoughts, feelings, and attitudes. In other words, we sacrifice our old way of relating to the world. Remember that the purpose of developing metta for these people is to make *yourself* calm and peaceful. To make others comfortable, first make *yourself* comfortable with them. It is not very easy, but in time we may see it is worthwhile—even natural!

PATIENCE, MINDFULNESS, AND METTA GO TOGETHER

Another traditional story about Sariputta from the Dhammapada shows how metta helps us overcome ill will. One day when Venerable Sariputta was on his alms round a brahmin and few of his friends saw him in the distance. They discussed how noble and patient Sariputta was. This brahmin said that he wanted to test Sariputta's patience, so he slowly went behind him and gave a very serious blow to Sariputta's back. Venerable Sariputta continued his alms round without even turning back to see who had struck him.

The brahmin felt so guilty that he rushed in front of Sariputta and apologized. When Sariputta asked him why he was apologizing, the brahmin said that he had given him a strong blow. Sariputta forgave him and continued his alms round. Then feeling even more guilty, the brahmin said, "Sir, if you really forgive me I would like you to come to my house and have your meal there." Accepting his invitation, Sariputta went to his house and after the meal gave him a Dharma talk.

Meanwhile the news spread around that a brahmin had struck Venerable Sariputta. Many people in the neighborhood gathered with clubs, sticks, and rocks to attack the brahmin. As soon as Sariputta finished his talk, he saw the people armed with all these weapons. Realizing what would happen to the brahmin, Sariputta used his mindfulness and compassion to help him. He gave his alms bowl to the brahmin and asked him to follow him. The angry people asked Sariputta to take his alms bowl back, yet he retorted, "Why?"

"Because we want to beat him up."

"Why?"

"Because he attacked you."

"I have forgiven him. You have not been attacked. So you all go home. This brahmin is a good man now."

After this episode the monks assembled in the discussion hall and started talking about this incident. Then the Buddha asked them what the topic of their discussion was. When they reported this incident, the Buddha said:

> One should not strike a brahmin
> And a brahmin should not set anger loose.
> Shame on the one who hits a brahmin
> And greater shame on the one who sets anger loose.
> For the brahmin, nothing is better
> Than restraining the mind
> From what it cherishes.
> Whenever one turns away from the intent to harm,
> Suffering is allayed.

We can learn from Sariputta's example and from the Buddha's teaching. Though it may be tempting to set anger loose, we may find that patience and loving-friendliness are essential for overcoming such emotions. If you find your patience tested, think of a person with only one eye—how his or her compassionate friends and relatives would do whatever they could to protect the one eye. Similarly, imagine there is a person who has great faith in practicing mindfulness but is always forgetful. Rather than getting angry, as a person practicing metta, protect this person's faith just as a compassionate person does everything possible to protect the sight of the one-eyed friend.

CHAPTER 9

Following Metta

METTA LEADS TO VIPASSANA

One who is practicing metta not only lives in peace and harmony but also learns to halt endless mental chatter and cut off the cycle of suffering. What this means is that if a person practices metta and gains tranquility, he or she can use that tranquility to gain concentration, which in turn leads to gaining insight. Thus metta practice is the basis of tranquility meditation and insight meditation. When you practice metta, you gain concentration faster. Concentration is an absolutely necessary part of insight or vipassana meditation. A concentrated mind can see impermanence, suffering, and nonself more clearly. Sharp concentration and insight allow one to see three moments of impermanence: the rising moment, the peak moment, and the passing-away moment. Rising is inconspicuous. The falling moment is a little clearer. The peak moment is also transforming and the most difficult to notice. With very sharp concentration and insight, however, we can notice all these three moments. Without good concentration we can't see the peak moment. We can only see the rising moment or the passing-away moment.

Keeping concentration on our object of meditation is difficult when our minds are not at peace. We can attempt to control for distractions in our environment, such as finding a quiet place to meditate or clearing our schedule, and we can eat a healthy meal so that hunger won't disturb us. Yet these do not account for inner distractions—our grasping at feelings and phenomena. When such thoughts arise we need patience and to abandon ill will. Developing metta is the best way to handle a mind that is impatient and angry. Remember that practicing metta begins with ourselves; when we are seated in meditation and judgmental thoughts arise, or thoughts of aversion or desire, if we feel a sense of warm friendliness for ourselves then we will become more tolerant and less frustrated both with ourselves and others. Loving-friendliness is in this way an important building block for our vipassana meditation.

A CLEAN PLACE TO STAND

Metta practitioners think not only of themselves, but also of others who share their surroundings. Such a person's presence is a blessing to all. Consider the following story from the commentary on the *Appamada Vagga*, the second chapter in the Dhammapada, ascribed to the great Indian scholar Buddhaghosa.

A long time ago there was man called Magha. He was working with other people at an unclean, dusty place in his village. He decided to clean a place for himself to stand. While he was working in the clean place, a selfish man pushed Magha out of his space and took his spot. Magha did not get upset. Instead he thought, "This man seems to like this clean spot. Let him have it and enjoy this clean place. I am glad I have been able to make him happy." Then he cleaned another spot and he continued his work while standing there. Another man, just as the one before, came along and took this place by pushing Magha out of the way. Magha was pleased, thinking, "This man, too, seems to like this clean spot. Let him have it and enjoy this clean place. I am glad I have been able to make him happy." Every time Magha cleaned a place and began to use it for himself, somebody would come and take it by pushing him out of his place. Magha thought, "This is very good that people are happy to stand on a clean spot. Let them enjoy the places that I clean. This is a very rare opportunity for me to do some service for this community." Then he went on cleaning the larger and larger areas to make people happy.

Magha went on cleaning roads. He made the roads smooth by removing big rocks, trimmed branches of trees that were obstructing the road, mended broken roads, and repaired dilapidated bridges. Seeing Magha laboring, another man asked him what he was doing. He said, "I am preparing my way to go to heaven."

This man asked him, "Can I join you?"

"Of course, you are welcome. The road to heaven is open to everyone. Come and join me," Magha said.

This man joined him. In a similar way, one by one, thirty-two more people joined Magha. This company of thirty-three people led by Magha went on cleaning roads, repairing roads, cleaning rivers, rebuilding broken bridges, and helping poor people build their homes. Their intention was to clean their villages for people to enjoy living in a clean environment.

One day, when they were engaged in their work in a certain village, the village headman asked them what they were doing. They explained to him that they were preparing the path to heaven. Thinking that the king would be disappointed with him for neglecting his duty of taking care of the area, the village headman feared he might lose his job and became angry. So he fabricated a story, compiled a list of false accusations, and complained to the king that some thieves were plundering the village. The king, without investigating properly, ordered his police to arrest these thirty-three people and bring them to him. Following the king's order the police arrested them and brought them to the king. Without any investigation the king imposed a severe punishment upon them—he ordered they be trampled to death by an elephant.

Magha said to his companions, "Friends, we should not hold any grudge against the man who has falsely accused us, nor against the king who imposed this severe punishment upon us. Our hearts are clean. We know we are doing something very wholesome. We are creating a very pleasant environment conducive to a very healthy and pleasant life. We are putting our metta into physical action. Anybody can see how healthy people are now. People appreciate what we are doing. We stand our ground. Don't give up your noble work. Don't get discouraged from your practice. We continue our remarkably wholesome act. Our defense is the metta practice. We don't have any other refuge. Metta is our matchless refuge, it will rescue us."

With thoughts of loving-friendliness in their minds, they remained calm and peaceful when the elephant was released to trample them. The village headman, leading the elephant on, was surprised when the elephant stopped and turned around to go back, and would not trample the thirty-three people. When the king learned about this he knew there must be a reason for the animal to turn around. He brought the thirty-three to him, and Magha and his companions informed the king that they were not thieves, but rather they had been cleaning the village, clearing a path to go to heaven. The elephant had thus seen and responded to the friendliness in their hearts in a way the village headman had not.

The king was thus very pleased. He gave them an entire village with the necessary facilities to live, and Magdha and his companions continued to do good deeds. They built a pilgrims' rest house in the village and lived there in peace for many years.

What this story shows us is that most important is our mental environment. When it is clean, our physical environment also becomes clean. Everyone likes a peaceful environment. As we have seen, when metta practitioners think not only of themselves, but also of others who share their surroundings, their presence becomes a blessing to all. Loving-friendliness creates a wholesome mind that in turn generates a wholesome environment. The *Discourse on Blessings* (*Mangala Sutta*) says living in a suitable location is itself a blessing. We can look to the source and see that thoughts of loving-friendliness create such an environment for ourselves and others.

Start Where You Are

We may feel that given the widespread suffering in the world, we need to have great wealth at our disposal to help those less fortunate than ourselves. The sheer scale of people living without electricity or running water or enough food to eat may feel overwhelming, like there is nothing we can do to make a difference in others' lives. But instead of throwing up our hands, we can think of the seemingly small things we actually *can* do to help others in our daily lives. Metta starts here—right where we are in this moment.

For example, one day I was in a taxi in Singapore. Seeing me in monk's robes the driver said, "Sir, if I had lots of money I could do a lot of good work."

"You don't need too much money to do good things," I said. "As you are driving your taxi, suppose you see an old woman trying to catch a taxi. You can stop for her. Open the door for her and help her get into your taxi. If you are a smoker, don't smoke while she is in your car. Speak gently and kindly to this lady. Drive her to her destination directly without taking her all around the city to charge her more. When you reach the destination come around and open the door for her. Holding her hand, walk her to the sidewalk and let her go with the sense of gratitude toward you."

I added, "When you do this you too will be very glad. Whenever you think of what you have done in addition to driving the taxi you will feel happy." You see, you can do all this without even an additional penny. You don't need money to have a good heart and practice metta.

When I travel sometimes I go to public bathrooms. If the bathroom is not clean, I clean it. On airplanes I clean the bathroom after I use it. I wish the next person coming to the bathroom will be pleased to see a clean toilet. Nobody knows who cleaned the toilet. I feel very glad to have done it.

Small things like this are in truth not small at all. They are ways to practice loving-friendliness every day.

CHAPTER 10

Fighting Fires with Metta

To use anger as your defense mechanism when you experience hardship is similar to the response an animal would have in the wild. We may feel that anger is a very natural response to difficulty—but where does that lead? As the Buddha says in the Dhammapada, "Hatred is never appeased by more hatred." An angry response only leads to more anger. Yet if you respond to anger with loving-friendliness, the other person's anger will slowly fade away. "By love alone is anger appeased," continues the verse in the Dhammapada. We can find a less reactive, more mindful way to handle hardship and suffering. We can respond from a place of wisdom instead of delusion or anger. In doing so, we will find that metta, not anger, is our best defense.

A true metta practitioner is like a firefighter who fights the fires of greed, hatred, and delusion. In the *Fire Sermon*, the Buddha said, "Our eyes, ears, nose, tongue, body, and mind are on fire. Visual objects, eye consciousness, eye contact, and feelings that arise dependent on contact—experienced as pleasant, unpleasant, or neutral—are all on fire. What fire? The fire of greed, hatred, and delusion, the fire of birth, growth, decay, death, sorrow, lamentation, grief, and despair."

Firefighters take care of themselves when they fight fires by wearing fire-resistant suits, and they undertake thorough training to become very skillful at their job. They also take all necessary precautions when they fight fires so they don't bring harm to themselves. Firefighters don't simply jump into their trucks when they hear the alarm. They rush to put on their protective suits and equipment and check the trucks before they take off, even though they inspect their fire trucks regularly.

Similarly, we should not take anything for granted and always be prepared to meet any situation with mindfulness and metta. We know we have the fire of greed, hatred, and delusion, the fire of hunger, thirst, grief, sorrow, lamentation, pain, and despair; these fires are burning day and night from the moment we are born until we die. We have smoldering slow-burning fires, quick and rapidly spreading fires, internal fires, external fires, deliberate fires, and spontaneous fires. Just as firefighters go through training so they can respond appropriately to each occasion, we practice mindfulness to become experts in recognizing fires and to build up our skill to be able to put them out.

Consider the story of Patacara, a woman who would become a revered elder nun in the Buddha's time. Before she became a nun, she lost her whole family in a single day. Because her husband, two young children, parents, and brother perished in a series of unfortunate accidents in that short period of time, Patacara was devastated. After years of wandering like a beggar, blinded by sadness, she came across the Buddha. He rescued her from the fire of sorrow, lamentation, pain, grief, and despair, first by helping her regain her presence of mind such that she could see clearly how another way of living was possible. Later on, when she was burning in the fire of passion, in grief for losing her family, the Buddha offered a teaching to rescue her from that fire. He shared with her the nature of impermanence, and the cooling balm of his loving-friendliness and wisdom extinguished Patacara's fire over time and helped her develop these qualities as well. With loving-friendliness, calmness, and mindfulness, we have the tools to put out the fires in our minds. Sometimes it is a constant struggle, but Patacara's story shows us that we too can experience peace when we open our minds and hearts to loving-friendliness. We have a natural, innate capacity for metta that no fire can destroy—and this metta itself is a powerful fire extinguisher!

We are not the only ones who benefit from loving-friendliness. When we protect ourselves from suffering and distress with metta, we also protect others and the environment. Similarly, when we protect others and the environment, we also protect ourselves. But change must start with us.

Firefighters wear protective gear in order to protect potential victims of fire. Doctors protect themselves from disease so that they can best keep their patients healthy. In case of a loss of cabin pressure aboard an airplane, parents put their own oxygen masks on first, and then put masks on their children. Taking care of ourselves like this is not selfish when we are developing metta. When we practice metta we protect our heart from being swept away from itself, and naturally we also help others protect themselves. Metta is our best defense because it protects both others and ourselves from the fires of mental harm.

CHAPTER 11

Relaxing into Forgiveness

Sometimes when we practice metta, pain, grief, and despair from the past will arise. Since we finally have space within our mind and heart, such unresolved or habituated emotions may come to the surface. Metta generates a relaxed state of mind that allows us to access that which is usually difficult to access. When this happens, see that you have a wonderful opportunity to train yourself to respond to your emotions with mindful awareness and love. If you observe your thoughts mindfully without trying to rationalize them, you will notice they change. Our relationship to our emotions is not static—we are not fixed to our pain, grief, or despair.

You can first feel a sense of ease by knowing that your painful emotions are not permanent. Notice that rigid thought patterns, habits that you have developed over the course of your life, have caused those feelings to strike up. Allow yourself to loosen up, accept the change, and let it go. Deepen your awareness of change and gradually you will feel more comfortable responding to emotions differently. The deeper your awareness of impermanence, the easier it is to practice metta.

As your awareness of change deepens, you can relax. This relaxation gives way to forgiveness, a beautiful side effect of practicing metta. Finally, you can forgive yourself for being hard on yourself for so long. You see that you were hard on yourself because of understandable causes and conditions. Because you did not pay attention to the subtle changes that had been taking place all along, you held on to old ways of handling pain. Now, as your understanding is deepening, you can learn to relax and forgive yourself. Your heart softens. To be able to extend thoughts of loving-friendliness to yourself is a very important part of metta practice.

Our metta then effortlessly expands like ripples in a pond, extending outward to others. Though their actions led you to feel hurt, gently relax your attitude toward the person or persons involved in creating the situation in which you suffered pain, which led to your grief and despair. Rather than force yourself to forgive them, observe with an open heart how they too have been conditioned by many factors over which they did not have any control. Neither you nor they are fully aware of those conditions—even if you try to discover all the conditions involved in making them behave the way they did in the past toward you at that particular time, you would never find all of the reasons. You can't necessarily know what caused you to be there in that moment, to be a victim of that situation. All you can do is take care of what you can do now. Having understood this reality, practice metta to yourself and for them. Then you may find that you are able to forgive the other person who caused your pain, grief, and despair.

We all have the seed for loving-friendliness in our hearts. All we need is the right conditions, the right soil and attention, to let it sprout, grow, and become strong. Each of us has the potential for metta to blossom in all our activities.

THE STORY OF ANGULIMALA

We can look to the story of Angulimala to find how we all—even those people we would least imagine—have a natural capacity for metta. In the Buddha's time, Angulimala was, to use the language of today, a serial killer, a mass murderer. He was so wretched that he wore around his neck a garland of fingers (which is what "anguli-mala" means) taken from the people he had slaughtered, and he planned to make the Buddha his thousandth victim. Despite Anguli-mala's reputation and his gruesome appearance, the Buddha none-theless could see his capacity for loving-friendliness. Thus, out of love and compassion—the Buddha's own metta—the Buddha taught the Dharma to this villainous murderer. As a result of the Buddha's teaching, Angulimala threw away his sword and surrendered to the Buddha, joining the followers of the Buddha and becoming ordained as a monk.

As it turned out, Angulimala was not by nature a cruel person, nor was he an evil person. In fact, he had been a kind boy, and murdered people out of a desire to follow a former teacher's instructions. In his heart, there was friendliness, gentleness, and compassion. As soon as he became a monk his true nature was revealed, and not long after his ordination, he became enlightened.

One day on his alms round Angulimala heard a woman groaning in labor pain. His heart melted. He went to the Buddha and reported that this woman was in pain. The Buddha asked him to go to the doorstep of her house and say to her, "Sister, since my birth I have not killed any living being. By the power of this truth may you deliver your baby without pain."

Angulimala said, "Venerable sir, how can I say that I have not killed any living being since my birth? I killed many people to add their fingers to my necklace."

"But that was before you were reborn as an arahant. Now you have overcome your ignorance, greed, and hatred. Now you are reborn as an arahant, a pure being, free from all defilement. Now you wish her to be free from pain and deliver her baby comfortably. Until your mind was free from all defilements you could not make this kind of wish," said the Buddha.

We all have experienced various conditions that combine in a unique manner to cause us to act in the ways we do—from a place of either frustration, love, anger, fear, or friendship. We cannot forget that we all have the seeds of loving-friendliness too. No one's heart has been hardened by these conditions to the extent that they are incapable of loving others and being kind to themselves. This is the nature of impermanence—our behavior is subject to change.

If the Buddha could help Angulimala forgive himself by seeing clearly his immense potential for awakening, you can surely find the kindness to forgive others—and even yourself.

CHAPTER 12

Communities of Metta

*A*s human beings we are naturally social creatures, and we
need others to live. When we are children we depend on
our families to survive, and when we are elderly perhaps our loved
ones give us a reason to get up every day. We are naturally driven
to be in relationship with others. Sometimes, though, this means
we look differently at those who are not part of our community and
think they do not deserve our kindness. Metta practice gives us the
opportunity to turn around that inclination so we feel warm-hearted
toward all beings, not just those we personally know and care for.
The Buddha told his first sixty disciples, "Go forth for the welfare of
the multitudes, for the happiness of the multitudes, out of sympathy
for the world for the benefit, welfare, and happiness of gods and
humans. Two should not go on one path. Teach the Dharma that is
beneficial in the beginning, beneficial in the middle, and beneficial
in the end." This is such a powerful demonstration of the Buddha's
immense love for all beings.

The Buddha advised his disciples to express their loving-
friendliness to people who give them support by teaching Dharma,
teaching meditation, and providing guidance. This way, metta is
magnified exponentially within communities, as more and more
people are able to learn to calm their minds and develop new strat-
egies for relating to others with loving-friendliness. Even in his last

days, the Buddha expressed his loving-friendliness for all beings by asking his disciples to practice what he taught.

In the Long Discourses (Digha Nikaya), the Buddha says:

> Monks, you should carefully assume those practices, which I have taught you for the sake of direct knowledge. You should practice them, cultivate them, and make much of them, so that this religious practice will last for a long time, will be standing. This is for the welfare of the multitudes, the happiness of the multitudes, the benefit, welfare, and happiness of gods and humans. This is out of sympathy with the world.

So you see, we practice mindfulness meditation and metta for all beings—this includes humans, non-humans, animals, gods, demons, ghosts, spirits, bipeds, quadrupeds, beings with hundreds of feet, thousands of feet, no feet, birds, and all beings in the water and air. We are part of a vast community with all beings, and the loving-friendliness we cultivate should extend to them as well.

In my own life, as a member of ordained communities, I have found that the entire monastic life depends on metta. The monastery is like a training ground for us to develop qualities like love and patience, and the community only functions well when each member practices metta. We are taught to be able to forgive any offense anybody commits against us. Loving-friendliness can help us avoid conflicts, especially due to misfortune and misunderstanding; it teaches us to be conciliatory and not proud or hostile. When one party feels hurt, friendliness can help establish peace and harmony. Monks and nuns should behave with patience and loving-friendliness in all physical, verbal, and mental actions—whether done in public or in private—toward our companions in monastic life. We should be very generous to share with our monastic community any knowledge and insight we have gained in our meditation practice. If a member of our community is lazy and does not participate in regular activities, we can advise him or her to do so without getting upset or angry. Our metta must be boundless—and our practice of patience must be boundless.

I have seen the benefit of this practice in my life—I have never regretted practicing metta and being patient. I never get tired of practicing metta and patience. Even if you do not live among monks and nuns (as most of you do not!), you will likely find that if you practice metta and patience with your companions you will not regret it either. Instead, you may be surprised to see that your kindness no longer becomes limited to those you interact with on a daily basis. Your metta can become limitless, and you may start to notice that you feel a warm heart for those who may have previously been outside your circle of care. The boundary that once limited who you feel a sense of friendliness toward gradually gets worn away, and any ill will you once harbored begins to disappear.

As we have seen, metta and mindfulness are often equated. Both have similar characteristics. As monks and nuns, in mindfulness practice we learn that we should cultivate clear comprehension while walking forward, going backward, looking away, wearing our robes, and carrying our alms bowl. Yet lay people can also train to live with such mindful awareness and clear comprehension in all their actions. We can develop our mindfulness while eating and drinking, while using the restroom, talking with others, observing silence, going to bed and rising in the morning, and while working and relaxing.

Similarly, we should practice metta in all these activities. Anger, resentment, or disappointment can arise at any time over the course of the day. We risk perpetuating our confused way of relating to others if we do not also make loving-friendliness a habit in all our encounters with others, even in the stories we tell ourselves about them.

Metta and mindfulness need commitment. We know that we suffer; we know all beings suffer. We practice metta to reduce our suffering and that of others. Ill will only maintains and nourishes suffering, but we should know that the root of metta is within us. If metta does not arise naturally for us, we must make a deliberate commitment to promote its development. It can become a new habit for us when we put forth the right amount of effort. We make all kinds of resolutions on special days—on holidays, anniversaries, and so forth—so we should also determine to practice metta on the special days in our life. We can make a birthday resolution to practice metta. But you don't have to wait until your birthday comes to make this commitment—even as you read these sentences, you can determine to make a mindful commitment to continue metta practice. This is mindfulness. This is mindful reflection.

So often we think that metta practice is beyond the reach of ordinary human beings, or perhaps that we don't have the time or capacity to practice. It's easy to assume that one must have a special, divine quality to understand the benefit of metta practice. It can be difficult for many of us to understand it, let alone practice it. Yet if you continue practicing metta you will see the benefit in your own life. One who sincerely seeks inner peace and happiness sees the power of loving-friendliness. This divine quality is deeply rooted in the human mind.

When you look around at your community, you may feel some disappointment, worry, or apprehension at the state of affairs. You see so much suffering—neighbors arguing, countries fighting, and children being neglected. Merely wishing for everyone to experience divine life on earth will not bring it about. However, we have the capacity to make this world heaven, beginning with how we interact in the world. This is called divinely living—to carry loving-friendliness in our hearts rather than ill will. Just as we can make hell on earth, metta practice can make heaven on earth. In the Numerical Discourses, the Buddha says:

> Here, Brahmin, when I am dwelling in dependence on a village or town, in the morning I dress, take my bowl and robe, and enter that village or town for alms. After the meal, when I have returned from the alms round, I enter a grove. I collect some grass or leaves that I find there into a pile and then sit down. Having folded my legs crosswise and straightened my body, I establish mindfulness in front of me. Then I dwell pervading one quarter with a mind imbued with loving-friendliness, likewise the second quarter, the third quarter, and the fourth quarter. Thus above, below, across, and everywhere, and to all as to myself, I dwell pervading the entire world with a mind imbued with loving-friendliness, vast, exalted, measureless, without enmity, without ill will. I dwell pervading one quarter with a mind imbued with compassion . . . with a mind imbued with altruistic joy . . . with a mind imbued with equanimity, likewise the second quarter, the third quarter, and the fourth quarter. Thus above, below, across, and everywhere, and to all as to myself, I dwell pervading the entire world with a mind imbued with equanimity, vast, exalted, measureless, without enmity, without ill will.
>
> Then, Brahmin, when I am in such a state, if I walk back and forth, on that occasion my walking back and forth is divine. If I am standing, on that occasion my standing is divine. If I am sitting, on that occasion my sitting is divine. If

I lie down, on that occasion this is my divine high and luxurious bed. This is that divine high and luxurious bed that at present I can gain at will, without trouble or difficulty.

Here the Buddha shows his gratitude to people in a village or town. Just as the residents support him by giving him sustenance on alms rounds, he generates boundless love for them and stretches his compassion out to the whole world. As he practices loving-friendliness for all beings in all quarters in the world, with mindfulness he lives in total peace. The Buddha understands the suffering in the world and practices metta for all suffering beings. He sees the suffering of all beings much better than any of us. Thus he is always full of loving-friendliness, compassion, appreciative joy, and equanimity. If we wish to see peace in the world we must also develop these qualities—we must let goodwill saturate our minds, because peace begins with each of us. The power of loving-friendliness, like the radiance of the sun, is beyond measure.

CHAPTER 13

Some Comments on the Metta Sutta

The *Metta Sutta* has been an integral part of my life since I became a monk. In my tradition, we recite this short text often and commit it to memory. During various difficult situations, verses from the *Metta Sutta* will come to my mind and I am able to remember to act with loving-friendliness. Even just reading it gives me a sense of peace, and you may feel the same way too. Let us now explore the meaning of the sutta to more fully understand it, which will help us firmly establish loving-friendliness in our lives. You may refer to the full sutta, the *Discourse on Loving-Friendliness*, in appendix 1, though we will attend to some passages below.

Metta practice purifies our minds. The first verses of the *Metta Sutta* give us a glimpse of the character of someone who has loving-friendliness in his or her heart and thus has a purified mind. We'll find that practicing metta changes our behavior at every level. Of course we can only do our own personal practice of metta, just as other people must do their own practice. And when we do so our mental patterns change over time. These thoughts are transformed into our speech and actions, which in turn affect other people.

The Buddha begins the discourse by saying, "This is what should be done by one who is skilled in goodness, and who knows the path of peace." When your mind is full of loving-friendliness, your mind is at peace. Over time you become less affected by previous conditions that would create negative thoughts of ill will. When your mind is at peace in this way, then you speak in a straight-forward and gentle manner, as the sutta points out. You begin to relate to the world differently—with patience, consideration, and understanding. People—and even animals!—naturally gravitate to you. They feel comfortable with you, and their minds are gentle and soft toward you.

Metta makes us stable and consistent in our actions because we do not feel stirred up by the changing winds of partiality. As we have seen, metta is not love as we might typically understand it—it is not based on whims, appearances, and others' attitudes toward us. Metta does not participate in the duality that causes you to feel kindly toward some beings and not others. Nor does it have an oppo-site—true loving-friendliness can never change into ill will or fear. Metta is a warm friendliness that leads you to be consistently kind to all beings, regardless of any circumstances. There is no place for discriminatory thoughts when we radiate a boundless, warm-hearted kindness from our hearts that has us wish for the well-being of all.

The sutta says metta practitioners are "Not proud and demanding in nature. Let them not do the slightest thing that the wise would later reprove." To consider what activities the wise would approve, we can look to how the Buddha treated those who wished to harm him. He felt no pride, no superiority to these beings. We saw in chapter 1 that he cultivated such powerful metta that he loved his bitterest enemy, Devadatta, who tried many times to kill him. Look-ing back to chapter 11 we find that he met with loving-friendliness even the highway robber and murderer Angulimala, who also wanted to kill him. He loved the fierce elephant, named Dhanapala, that Devadatta sent to trample him. The Buddha loved all of these beings the same way he loved his own son, Rahula. When Devadatta died on his way to see the Buddha, monks asked the Buddha what his future would be. The Buddha answered that he would become enlightened in the future. That is the kind of loving-friendliness, guided by mindfulness, that allows us to live in peace and harmony. That is the character that we can aspire to have. It is certainly possible to achieve.

Weak or strong, seen or unseen, far or near, born or coming to birth—all should be included in our net of loving-friendliness. We make the heartfelt wish, "In gladness and in safety, may all beings be at ease."

The sutta brings our attention to how there are beings that are seen and those that are unseen. We normally think of beings that we have seen or heard, and it is easier to practice metta toward the beings that we can see. It is not that easy to practice metta toward beings that we don't see. This is the reason we should ignore the distinctions between beings, because in the face of metta all are the same. It doesn't matter whether we have seen the other beings or not. All we know is that they exist in the world—they can be visible or invisible. There are all kinds of invisible beings that suffer. That they don't know how to get rid of their suffering should inspire our warm-hearted feeling toward them.

In your metta practice, you may find it is not easy to visualize those that we have not seen. It is not impossible, however, for us to think of the countless beings we have seen—relatively speaking, we only have seen very few. Those we have not seen are much greater in number. This is why this practice is called boundless. If we were to put a limit on our metta, where should our boundary line be? When we cultivate boundless metta our friendliness should not have a limit in time and space. We don't know the kind of suffering those who are apart from us are going through, let alone the suffering of unseen beings. We don't know what kind of dangers and calamities await them. There are countless uncertainties in life—anything can happen to anybody. We wish them all peace. In order to cover all beings that we have seen and not seen, we simply cultivate this noble thought in our minds. If something inevitable happens, let them have courage and determination to meet and overcome the situation.

Whether beings are far or near doesn't make any difference. Even all the microbes living on our bodies should be considered among the beings that live near to us. Their suffering is the same. The main difference between those who are near and far is we can witness the suffering of those that are near us whereas we don't see the suffering of those that are far away. There are beings out of sight in faraway places, and their number could be much more than those that are close to us. Far and near also applies to the emotional distance we may feel to some people and animals. When we dearly love somebody, for instance, we say, "He or she is close to my heart." Similarly, when we don't like someone very much we say, "I keep him or her at arm's length." We should make effort to include even these beings in our metta practice, without any distinction whatsoever. The common denominator for all of us together is that we suffer. Metta practice includes everyone, omitting none. This includes even arahants! For our purposes it is inconsequential that they have attained full enlightenment by eliminating the cause of suffering and are free from suffering, sorrow, lamentation, grief, and despair. In order to complete this all-encompassing metta practice even they are included. This indeed is our wish.

While we are practicing metta many animals may be slaughtered around the world. This is something we have no control over. Even the Buddha did not have any control over the killing of animals and human beings in his time. For fifty years a neighboring farmer slaughtered pigs near the place where the Buddha and his monks lived. The Buddha neither asked him to stop killing pigs nor did he seek the help of his very powerful supporter, King Kosala, to stop the killing of the pigs. There is no need to get upset and angry with people who kill—even they need our loving-friendliness. Rather, we wish them to be free from the greed, hatred, and ignorance that blind them to the truth that all beings fear death. Metta is an individual practice that others cannot be forced to participate in. We may not have any power to stop them from killing living beings, but we ourselves should neither kill nor intentionally support the killing of living beings.

Again, returning to the sutta, we wish all beings to be at ease: the seen and the unseen, and those living near and far away. It is easy to practice metta to those beings that are near us, like our parents, relatives, and friends. They are near to us in space and they are near to our heart. We love our dogs, cats, and other pets. We can easily send our metta to them. When distance separates us we think of them very dearly and send our metta to them. How easy it is to forget others who are not close to us in space and not close to our heart—yet we can send our metta to them too. As we don't know their situation, we should include them in our metta practice and wish for their well-being and happiness.

Our metta practice should include all that are born or coming to birth. There are beings that are still seeking birth, in the process of coming out of their mothers' wombs or eggs. This is another marvelous aspect of metta practice—it encompasses everyone.

The *Metta Sutta* goes on to say, "Let none deceive another, or despise any being in any state. Let none through anger or ill will wish harm upon another." Here the Buddha advises us not only to abstain from deceiving others, but also to wish that others not deceive one anyone else. While we practice honesty we may wish that others also practice honesty. This is a very wholesome wish that we can all make—for everybody to be free from suffering.

The metta practitioner should not wish anyone to suffer for any reason. Greed, hatred, and delusion lead people to commit so much harm. They cause people to look down on others' weaknesses or look at some people with contempt, even to cheat or kill. A mind full of metta does not cultivate such a harmful attitude, because it sees all beings as equal. Wishing others success causes us no harm. Just as the sun dispels darkness, loving-friendliness destroys the darkness of hatred. If a disdainful thought should arise, the metta practitioner becomes mindful of it quickly and adjusts his or her attitude accordingly.

The Buddha later says in the *Metta Sutta*, "Whether standing or walking, seated or lying down, free from drowsiness, one should sustain this recollection." Sometimes meditation may be misinterpreted to be a kind of practice that makes the meditator a heartless or indifferent being, a robot without any love and compassion for other living beings. We must remember, however, that the Buddha has strongly advised us to cultivate four sublime states of mind: loving-friendliness, compassion, appreciative joy, and equanimity. We can also maintain recollection of metta through all our activities, as this verse suggests. When we do so, being mindful is far from being indifferent or heartless. In all of our activities we may discover we become more kind, gentle, and considerate.

Mindful observation of our own individual mental states can make us aware of how some thought waves are harmful, destructive, and painful. Others are peaceful and joyful. Then our mind rejects that which is harmful and cultivates that which is peaceful and joyful. We can't truly learn this from books, teachers, friends, or even enemies—we can only learn this from our own practice and experience. When harmful thoughts arise we learn not to entertain them, and when peaceful thoughts arise we let them grow and stay in the mind much longer. This way we learn from our own experience how to think more healthily. This practice conditions our minds to grow loving-friendliness. This means that peaceful thought waves appearing in our mind by themselves can be generated at will later on.

This practice helps us to comprehend that loving-friendliness does grow in the backyard of our own mind.

CHAPTER 14

Stories of Loving-Friendliness

*I*n this chapter, I'd like to share a number of stories about simple places in my life where I have seen the functioning of loving-friendliness. If some of the stories seem unremarkable, I hope this will serve to help you see how simple, in a certain way, the attitude of loving-friendliness is, and how it might be included in many aspects of your own everyday life.

When we bought the first thirteen acres of land in West Virginia to establish the Bhavana Society, some friends asked, "Bhante, why on earth did you choose West Virginia to buy land for a retreat center? It's not an atmosphere supportive of Buddhadharma."

It may not have been an easy choice, but we did our best. We went door-to-door introducing ourselves to our neighbors. The family on the property closest to us could not accept us being there. I was naive and said, "When we start the center, please come meditate with us whenever you like."

My neighbor was seriously offended and said, "You do any damn thing you want. I am a Christian!" That was exactly what my friends had warned me about. And for years afterward, that neighbor gave us lots of problems.

We began inviting our friends for retreats, and sometimes twenty to thirty people would come. Even before we had any buildings, we meditated sitting on the ground under the trees. I instructed everyone to practice metta meditation, to send thoughts of loving-friendliness wholeheartedly and not let resentment enter their minds. This neighbor's house was about fifty yards from the grove where we were sitting, and he and his wife started singing Christian hymns loudly to disturb us. But we enjoyed their singing. The woman's voice was sweet and she sang beautifully.

The next time we meditated, they played drums using loudspeakers. They thought that the drumbeats would come only in our direction, but the sound dispersed all around and the other neighbors were disturbed. They telephoned the sheriff, who came and stopped it. So the next time we meditated, they shouted in the middle of the night. Again, we did not respond. So they fired a high-powered rifle in the middle of the night to scare the retreatants, but we never complained.

We had a mailbox at the entrance to our land. It was shot at. We used duct tape to cover bullet holes and continued to use the mailbox. Then it was clubbed. We still used it. Then it was uprooted and thrown away. We did not do anything in response. Then dog excrement was put in it. When the mail carrier came and put the mail inside he saw the excrement. So we bought another mailbox, which was then damaged in the same way.

Then our neighbors spread the rumor we were eating their dogs. They said they had lost eight dogs. Another neighbor told them, "They're vegetarians. They don't even eat meat, how could they kill your dogs?"

They circulated a petition against us, but the other neighbors refused to sign, telling them that Buddhists are peaceful people they wanted to welcome to the neighborhood and not drive away.

Our hostile neighbors had four small children. The parents encouraged them to throw stones at us, spit at us, and use foul language to insult us. The children did that.

One winter, there was a lot of snow and it was very cold. These neighbors didn't have enough firewood to heat their home. We invited them to come and take firewood from us. In spite of all the things they'd done to us, they took the firewood, and continued with their ways for another seven years. After that, the husband went away; we don't know where. We never saw him again. Then the children grew up and went away.

A few years later, the eldest son returned to the Bhavana Monastery as an adult and apologized. He said, "When we were little, we didn't know anything. We did what our father asked us to do. I joined the navy and discovered that Buddhism is a peaceful religion. So I've come to say I'm very sorry for everything we did to you."

We accepted his apology and made him feel comfortable. We were pleased with this young man and wished him success in his search for truth.

I tell this story because metta practice is not easy. Sometimes it takes a great deal of patience to practice loving-friendliness.

Now we have no shooting or drumming or shouting. All those years we sent metta five times a day—during early morning meditation, breakfast time, lunchtime, evening puja time, and evening meditation time.

Perhaps sending all that metta eventually helped things on our neighbor's side. But I know it helped us!

My dog, Brown, and I often went out walking. He was a big, beautiful dog, very gentle and friendly, full of metta. Other dogs came and attacked him, yet he never fought, even with small dogs. Whenever other dogs attacked Brown and me, I sent every ounce of metta to those dogs. If that didn't work, I'd use my metta stick. I struck the road with my stick to stop them from attacking Brown or me—of course I would never hit the dogs. Normally, the dogs wouldn't come close to me because of the stick. These were fierce dogs, showing their teeth and trying to bite. When I showed them my stick, they stopped coming at me. Wielding metta with the stick was enough. That was all I had to do.

After we were together many years, Brown was hit by lightning and paralyzed. The veterinarian wanted to put him to sleep. Instead two community members put him between their beds and stroked him all night long, giving him water to drink. They took care of Brown the whole night. The next morning he passed away peacefully.

This too is part of how we practice loving-friendliness.

The Bhavana Society is in a rural area where the main sights are deer, squirrels, birds, wild turkeys, skunks, possums, groundhogs, foxes, and snakes. A few miles away from our center is a big apple orchard and apple-packing factory.

I was curious to see how they pack apples. So one day I asked one of our Bhavana residents to drive me there. As we approached, we saw five people getting out of their trucks and cars to start work. When they saw me in my orange robe, they began to giggle, looking at me with an expression of contempt and saying some funny things. With a lot of metta in my heart, I straightaway approached the man who looked like the leader and with a friendly smile, I said, "Sir, I live in this neighborhood. Originally I am from Sri Lanka. I've never seen an apple-packing plant, would you mind showing it to me?" As soon as I said this, he stopped giggling and became friendly.

Then he said, "Yes, sir, I'll be very glad to show you around. Come with me."

Since I didn't have any fear of these people, I was able to approach them, and after that they became friendly toward me. He showed me the entire facility, spending almost an hour explaining all aspects of the operation. Then he sent me off with a friendly "Y'all come back now, ya hear?"

In 1993, I traveled to Europe. Before I left, my good friends at the monastery advised me to be careful. "Ruffians might harass you," they said. "As you are traveling alone, they might insult you or even try to hurt you."

"I am a simple monk and a small person," I said. "Why would anyone want to hurt me?"

I have the "weapon" the Buddha gave the monks who went to meditate in the forest: loving-friendliness. I trust in that weapon. I thought, "So long as I go with that weapon, no one will hurt me."

I've met many people on trains and buses throughout Europe. Whenever I was trying to put my bag in an overhead compartment or under a seat, someone always helped me. When I got down from trains, buses, or airplanes, people helped get my bags from where they were stored. Doing all this, they showed their metta. And I met it with my own.

One day I was walking in Hamburg, a port city on the Baltic and North Seas. I saw six or seven teenagers sitting and drinking beer. As soon as they saw me, they began to jeer. Then as I passed them, they invited me to join them for a beer.

"Thank you very much," I said. "Not now. Maybe some other time! Enjoy yourselves and have nice day"—and I walked away. On my way back, they were still there. This time they did not invite me. They just smiled and went on enjoying themselves. They did not harass me. I simply felt friendly with them.

There are people who don't want to hear about loving-friendliness. Once I was invited to lead a retreat in Poland. The woman who invited me asked, "Do you teach metta meditation?"

"Yes," I said.

"I hate metta," she said.

I went there and taught a ten-day metta retreat. By the end of the retreat, she loved metta meditation.

If you don't feel like loving-friendliness practice is for you, perhaps you are like this Polish woman. The alternative to turning away is really diving in. This too is the path to loving-friendliness.

A friend put a log at the top of the hill along my regular Back Creek Road walking path for me to sit on when I take a rest and drink some water. One day, after several years of walking along this path and sitting on the log, the young man who lives in the house across the road from that log drove by in his van. As he turned in toward his house, he stopped his van and pointed toward a folding chair with armrests leaning against a tree on his land and said, "Can you see that chair?"

"Yes," I said.

"That chair is for you to sit down and drink your water. You don't have to sit on that log anymore. From now on, you sit on this chair while you have your water and relax comfortably."

It was a wonderful feeling! I'd been seeing him since he was ten or twelve years old. And he'd been watching me walk on this road for about eighteen years. Each time I saw him, I waved and asked, "How are you?"

"I am fine, and you?" he would say.

"Okay. Have a nice day," I'd say.

"Same to you," he'd reply, and we would part.

Several years after that, I was walking with a friend. When we came to the place where the chair was, I sat in the chair and began to drink water. My friend was standing. Seeing us, the young man brought another chair and invited him to sit down. A couple of years later, I was walking with two people. Two of us were sitting and the third was standing, and the young man brought another chair.

Now there were three chairs leaning against a tree in his front yard, placed there intentionally for our use.

This is how he showed his metta to my friends and me. When you practice metta, you create an opportunity for others to practice as well. Everyone has the potential to practice loving-friendliness. We support one another. This is metta in action. Don't underestimate the power of any little word you share or any tiny thing you do to make someone happy. Metta begets metta. Love begets love.

CHAPTER 15

Ecology and Loving-Friendliness

*E*cological and environmental concerns are inherent in Buddhism. We can extend loving-friendliness and compassion beyond people and animals to include plants and the earth itself. Practicing metta can have a profound effect on the environment. Scholar, translator, and American Buddhist monk Bhikkhu Bodhi writes:

> With its philosophical insight into the interconnectedness and thoroughgoing interdependence of all conditioned things, with its thesis that happiness is to be found through the restraint of desire in a life of contentment rather than through the proliferation of desire, with its goal of enlightenment through renunciation and contemplation, and its ethic of non-injury and boundless loving-friendliness for all beings, Buddhism provides all the essential elements for a relationship to the natural world characterized by respect, care, and compassion.

The scholar Lily de Silva adds, "The *Karaniyametta Sutta* enjoins the cultivation of loving-friendliness towards all creatures timid and steady, long and short, big and small, minute and great, visible and invisible, near and far, born and awaiting birth. All quarters are to be suffused with this loving attitude. Just as one's own life is precious to oneself, so is the life of the other precious to himself. Therefore a reverential attitude must be cultivated towards all forms of life." It's easy to see how this attitude naturally has an impact on how we interact with and care for the environment.

We can make a conscious effort to keep the environment clean and beautiful so other living beings—humans and animals—will live in peace and enjoy what is there. Every tiny, living being contributes to ecological balance. Practicing metta, we can keep roads, rivers, streams, and forests clean. Keeping the environment clean, we make people happy. All this is a part of our metta practice. This is loving-friendliness in action.

When we use natural resources carefully, we are practicing metta. If we protect our surroundings, we protect everyone's health. Our metta supports everyone. We should be prudent in using resources. If we continue to abuse and pollute the environment, the earth will become unsuitable for the future. With deep metta for current and future generations, the Buddha said, "Destroy the forest of defilements, but don't cut trees." When we keep roads and forests clean, we practice loving-friendliness.

For each of us, metta practice is an individual—not collective—practice. We can share our loving-friendliness experience with other people, but we must each cultivate it in our own hearts.

Loving-friendliness can lead us to discover ways that let us interact with the environment less harshly.

For all of us, the changing climate is an issue of pressing concern. Geological engineers and environmentalists are coming up with many very difficult yet beneficial proposals to slow or stop climate change. Yet in addition, if we all honestly practice metta we too can help protect this world, with its trillions of living beings. We protect our environment and all living beings—even future generations—when we have loving-friendliness.

I see metta in action in the example of compassionate farmers in Sri Lanka who share their crops with birds. When they harvest their crops they leave a small part for birds. Some farmers have even learned to repel insects without harmful chemicals. They collect herbal plants, pound them, and extract juice from them. When they irrigate their crops, as water starts running they pour this juice into the mouth of the irrigation channel. The water covers the rice field with this juice, which puts out a certain odor to repel insects. The insects don't like the smell of this juice and stay away without being harmed.

I know a man in Brazil who collects bee venom for making medicine without killing bees. He gets a glass tube about three inches wide by two feet long and connects it to tiny electric wires. These wires are connected to a car battery. He places this glass right at the entrance of the beehive. When the bees come and sit on it they feel the warmth of the glass. Then they sting the glass and enter the hive, leaving the venom on the glass. After some time—maybe a week or so—he scrapes the dry bee venom into a container and fills small bottles. This is a very good metta practice.

Although not many of us keep bees, we can still think of where we can put our efforts into making changes to benefit the earth and protect animals and plants—especially when it comes to how much energy we waste every day. Innovative environmentally conscious people have produced energy-saving light bulbs, and we can save a lot of energy using them. We can also save energy by turning off electricity when we don't need it instead of leaving lights on in our homes and outdoors around our houses. To make such things a habit takes mindful awareness and even keeping thoughts of loving-friendliness in our minds.

As a consequence of cutting down the forests, we destroy animal habitats. In Sri Lanka, elephants are in danger because of the clearing of the forest. Not only elephants but also numerous other animals are frequenting villages, causing conflicts with humans. Many animals and plants are now extinct or endangered. Even the insects that pollinate our crops are threatened and need our protection. We humans have a great moral responsibility to protect life with loving-friendliness for future generations. On our land we even collect dead branches and pile them up for little animals—squirrels, mice, snakes, rabbits, foxes, possums, baby deer, and porcupines—to hide in when chased by predators. This is an act of metta, just as protecting endangered species is an act of metta. When we practice loving-friendliness we not only minimize our hatred, but also reduce our greed for overusing and abusing the environment.

There are wonderful people around the globe engaged in cleaning and protecting the environment. There are people who go around cleaning rivers. One friend of ours removed thousands of tires, microwaves, refrigerators, cans, bottles, toasters, shoes, and countless other items carelessly thrown into the Chesapeake & Ohio Canal, a scenic area outside of Washington, DC. Another neighbor collects bottles, cans, plastic containers, and numerous other items people have thrown on the road. We encourage our monastics to collect trash from the roadside when they walk. Out of compassion, not out of fear of punishment, we should all refrain from throwing trash onto the road while driving.

These are all ways of practicing metta, all activities done from the spirit of loving-friendliness.

Think of ways you can practice metta in action within the limited time and space of your life. It takes time, determination, and touching the space within your heart.

CHAPTER 16

Some Tips for Living a Life of Loving-Friendliness

In this section, I'd like to offer a small selection of tips for living a life of metta, of loving-friendliness. I'll talk especially about the ways these tips can help with overcoming negative mental habits.

1. Be Careful of Anger

I'm sure that sometimes you are angry with yourself.

And if you're like most people that I know, it is possible that you are too hard on yourself. Perhaps you expect perfection of yourself. And perhaps when you expect perfection of yourself, very often you can get angry with yourself. If you expect to be perfect, since you are not perfect, you'll get angry. It is of utmost importance that you cultivate compassion toward yourself, cultivate loving-friendliness toward yourself. This can soften your heart. When your heart is soft you learn to take things easy and accept your own imperfections and shortcomings without getting angry.

When you are gentle and compassionate toward yourself you can see how much suffering you have caused when you were harsh and rigid. Through compassion toward yourself, you learn to be compassionate toward others who are as imperfect as you are. You can see that they are not different from you. Realizing the imperfection of others helps you to understand people's shortcomings and to restrain yourself from getting angry. Understanding that you have committed many offenses when you were unmindful helps you to forgive others' offenses. When you come to a better understanding of your own life, you can forgive others easily and reduce your anger.

When you know somebody is angry with you, rather than reacting from anger, practice loving-friendliness. Rather than causing more harm with your anger, consider doing some small act of kindness. Perhaps you might offer a gift or a favor, or offer to help someone in difficult times. It is not difficult to speak in consoling and comforting language to help another deal with a difficult situation. You will be glad that you helped this angry person and they will be glad that you do not hold a grudge against them. By opening the door to your heart with loving-friendliness, they might even regret that they offended you. This could be the occasion for both of you to apologize and reestablish your friendship.

If you don't work with your anger with care and loving-friendliness, and instead throughout your life you just strengthen the habit of being angry, you greatly increase the likelihood that when it comes time for you to die, you will do so in a state of anger, of great mental anguish.

Recalling that we all die, that the fact of death is certain even though the time of death is uncertain, we can reorient to living this short life in peace, harmony, and loving-friendliness. And this is true regardless of any stance about rebirth.

As the Buddha said to the people of Kalama: "Suppose there is no life after death; due to your practice of loving-friendliness, you will enjoy this life. Suppose there is a life after death; then, because of your loving-friendliness meditation, you will be reborn in a peaceful place. If there is no life after death, you will suffer from your anger here and now. If there is life after death, you will suffer again in the next life."

2. Don't Blame Anybody

Most of the time, an angry person blames someone else for their anger. We can see this practice mostly among narrow-minded or immature persons. Children are a good example. When two children are caught in an angry argument one will say, "I didn't start it. They started it! They insulted me."

The other child will, of course, say the same thing. Being afraid of punishment, they might even lie in anger. Even as adults some people quickly accuse others for their anger. I have heard many grownups say, "It is not my fault. I do everything possible to avoid conflict and argument. But *they* always do something or another to make me angry." If you want to live a life of loving-friendliness, don't blame others for what arises in your mind.

Nor should you blame yourself for your anger. Blame is completely unnecessary. Instead of blaming, look at anger impartially—just see it arising, and don't act from it. Act instead from your highest intentions, your metta. You must look at anger impartially not only at the time when you are angry, but especially at times when you are *not* angry.

When you are angry, you always think it is the other person who is wrong and made you angry. It is easy to fall into this trap of believing our own stories. It is so hard for us to really penetratingly see through our own anger—it takes a great deal of mindfulness.

Like anything else, anger arises not independently, but dependently, due to causes and conditions. Apparent causes may be immediate or remote—and sometimes the causes of anger may not be apparent at all. If you do not find the cause of your anger, don't worry about it. Without trying to justify your anger, simply pay attention to it and look at it with the eye of wisdom. Looking at it with mindfulness helps you to understanding its impact on your mind and body.

Mindfulness is essential. Blame is unnecessary.

3. Try to Cultivate Gratefulness

Try to cultivate gratefulness to your parents, teachers, relatives, friends, and even strangers who have done any little good thing for you, recently or even in the distant past. Our habitual tendency is to look past all the good things others have done for us and to instead focus on and replay every real or imagined slight. Finding time in your life to actively cultivate gratefulness is an important part of the practice of loving-friendliness.

Gratefulness softens your heart and helps reduce your anger—and gratefulness seeds the soil to allow loving-friendliness to grow naturally into joy and peace.

4. Choose Your Friends Wisely

The people we spend our time with have a great impact on our mind, so we should take care in making these decisions. The Buddha emphasized the importance of good spiritual friends, friends devoted to wisdom and loving-friendliness. On one particular occasion, Ananda, who was the Buddha's attendant, came to the Buddha and said that in his view half the spiritual life had to do with spiritual friendship. The Buddha immediately corrected him and said, "Do not say this, Ananda! Spiritual friendship is not *half* the spiritual life. It's the *entire* spiritual life!"

Choosing to spend time with angry people can be very damaging to your own state of mind and it can serve to reinforce your own habit of anger. If instead you can help such people through your practice of loving-friendliness, you should of course help them. Otherwise, when possible and appropriate, it is often best not to associate with them.

When people habitually indulge in anger, they destroy their opportunity to live in the peace and harmony that using their luminous mind could bring. They destroy their growth along the spiritual path.

When I say this, sometimes people ask: "How about your compassion toward somebody full of hatred? If you are so full of loving-friendliness, shouldn't you help that person?" But for all of us who are not enlightened, we must honestly and mindfully assess how much we could help. Our capacity is limited. As an unenlightened person, you have your own limitations. When you hit the edge of your limitation, you yourself may get very nervous, very tense, uptight, and rigid. Eventually, you may be very much like that angry person.

However, perhaps your own son, daughter, brother, sister, mother, father, uncle, or cousin is a very angry person. How can you not associate with them? Your daughter needs your help. Your son needs your help. They all need your help. As a responsible person you cannot simply ignore them. Therefore use their temper as an opportunity for you to cultivate metta with patience. When others are angry we should try not to get angry, but remain calm and peaceful.

Relatedly, in the *Discourse on Blessings*, the Buddha said, "Not to associate with foolish persons is a blessing."

An angry person may have great book knowledge, great experience, but cannot take care of their own negative emotions. They do not use their intelligence properly—and this is a kind of foolishness.

5. *Look Honestly at Yourself*

Honest and mindful introspection is essential for truly integrating a life of loving-friendliness. You must be willing to look at yourself, at your own motivation—especially when you experience anger and greed.

When those things arise, and your mindfulness allows you to notice those things have arisen, really ask yourself, "Am I acting selfishly?" We all have a tendency to have a deep and unexamined belief that things should go the way we want them to—and from this we end up acting as if everything must be done "my own way"—"my way or the highway!"

The alternative is to act from a place of harmony and cordiality, and to look for ways to compromise. The Buddha's path is, after all, called the Middle Way!

So look honestly at the state of your own mind—look for where you may be falling into extremes, into purely self-centered behavior—and use mindful metta to return to the Middle.

6. Do Some Physical Exercise

Physical exercise relaxes the body and mind. When the muscles are relaxed circulation becomes very good. Then tension and uptightness fade away. If we exercise every day as a habit, it helps us to overcome our anger and practice metta. The act of doing something very concrete and physical can be an important tool we use to help ourselves let go of difficult mind states that may have arisen.

7. Do Some Mental Exercise

Mental exercise is, in a certain sense, just another name for *right effort*, one of the steps on the eightfold path. It may sound very technical and very abstract when you read about skillful effort in books—but when we put it into action it becomes very practical. Doing the mental exercise of metta each day is right effort. Reminding yourself each morning of the shortcomings of anger and your commitment to not give in to it is right effort.

As the mind is fresh in the morning, an early morning commitment stays in the mind longer and more strongly than the mental commitment you make any other time of the day. If you do your mental exercise, if you repeat the commitment every morning, eventually you will remember throughout the rest of your day. Let your commitment to overcome anger and live from metta become a habit.

Having made this determination, your anger will weaken and eventually will diminish.

This is not suppression. This is a mindful and deliberate commitment with understanding that helps you minimize your anger and maximize your loving-friendliness.

CHAPTER 17

Eight Mindful Steps to Metta

Truly it is the case that metta permeates the teachings of the Buddha. Loving-friendliness is implicit in the Four Noble Truths, the Buddha's first and most basic teaching. The fourth noble truth is the path of eight mindful steps to happiness. The second of these steps, skillful thinking, includes cultivating generosity, loving-friendliness, and compassion. Only when we put metta into action does it perform miracles.

Each of the eight mindful steps to happiness, often called the noble eightfold path, begins with the word *skillful* (*samma*), also translated as "right" or "complete." These eight steps are a way to overcome suffering and realize joy through the cultivation of wisdom and morality. In each step is the practice of loving-friendliness. Thus, in an important way, we could also call the eightfold path "eight mindful steps to metta."

1. We practice metta through skillful understanding—comprehending dissatisfaction, its causes, the end of these causes, and the path to happiness.
2. We practice metta through skillful thinking—letting go of greed, hatred, and thoughts of cruelty.
3. We practice metta through skillful speech—refraining from lying, slanderous or harsh talk, and gossip.

4. We practice metta through skillful action—abstaining from killing, stealing, and committing sensual or sexual misconduct.

5. We practice metta through skillful livelihood—not taking up a livelihood that is inherently harmful to others or ourselves.

6. We practice metta through skillful effort—overcoming negative tendencies and arousing and developing wholesome actions.

7. We practice metta to develop skillful mindfulness. Metta practice is itself mindfulness.

8. We practice metta to gain skillful concentration. Metta meditators attain *jhana*, a profoundly concentrated state of mind.

Each of the eight mindful steps begins and ends with the practice of metta and brings us closer to becoming fully integrated into everyday life. These steps are meant as a guideline, to be considered, contemplated, and practiced—in short, they are to be lived. It can be said that Buddhism is a process of self-discovery—and this certainly includes discovering our own capacity as a loving, kind, and friendly being.

The meaning of *samma* ("skillful," "right," "complete") includes an ethical aspect and a balanced, middle way of being. When things go "right," we often experience a felt sense that confirms that this is the correct decision or action—and the correct way of holding open the heart and mind with regard to the world.

Three Modes of Metta

There are three levels, three modes, of metta practice: speaking, thinking, and feeling. And these three modes are also related to the elements of the eightfold path.

Recitation, the speaking mode, comes first. Practicing right speech, we say what we mean and mean what we say—and we bring this same approach to our metta practices.

When we recite the metta phrases, we might be tempted to only think them to ourselves, silently—but it can be quite helpful to do it audibly. At the time of the Buddha, teachings were recited aloud and memorized—and this is the way they were kept alive and handed down. It's truly a powerful way to engage with teachings. Moreover, when you hear your own voice speaking these important words, you're more likely to remember them later and more able to call them to mind in challenging situations. Then, in relaxed moments, you may discover you naturally repeat what you are learning by memory. It's like singing a favorite song in the shower. Children naturally repeat lyrics and other things they've learned by heart. When we are relaxed, the words just come up. Practicing metta in this way, you may discover that, more and more, loving-friendliness just naturally comes up.

Verbal recitation includes speech in daily life. Practicing right speech, we must be mindful when we speak to communicate our intention clearly and skillfully. One way we can ensure our intentions in speaking are wholesome is to allow the mind to generate metta, to touch loving-friendliness, in the moment before we open our mouths.

When I was in Malaysia, a few children came to the temple every evening to play. I composed some passages on metta and invited them to recite them with me in the shrine room. The children memorized the passages and I heard them reciting the words while they were playing. Their parents were delighted. Now, fifty years later, some of these children are grandparents and still remember those passages. And more importantly, they still practice metta. I'm sure all the grandchildren can tell!

In the second level of practice, silent reflection, we think about what we have been reciting, always working to deepen our understanding of what it means to live a life of loving-friendliness.

In the *Discourse on Two Kinds of Thought* there is a story about the Buddha before his enlightenment. The Buddha-to-be gained concentration by thinking and talking to himself, mindfully like a cowherd guides cows with a stick. When he guides his cows to the pen, he uses a stick to direct his cows in the right direction. Whenever one of them goes astray, he gently pokes her and makes her rejoin the herd. Similarly, when we talk or think we should not let our mind go astray. Use mindfulness at that time to put the mind on the right track.

The way we use our minds matters; the way we think and talk to ourselves has a major impact on what we express, communicate, and even perceive. What we think becomes a habit. If we are always complaining about others or rehearsing our grievances and difficulties, we are strengthening the anger habit. What we express is what we have in mind. If we condition our thoughts in loving ways, our words will be loving—indeed, our experience of the world will be more loving. Practicing metta, we create a loving atmosphere around us. Reflecting on loving-friendliness, thinking the phrases of metta frequently, is actually like cultivating a new habit of mind, gradually counteracting all the habitual greed and anger we've habitually rehearsed for so long. This level of practice is related to right intention in the eightfold path.

The third level of practice is assimilating the meaning and feeling of loving-friendliness into our own lives. When we think angry thoughts, we feel angry and unhappy. Is this not so? When we think loving thoughts, we feel loving and joyful and our acts are kind.

The Buddha spoke about this in the Dhammapada:

> All actions are led by the mind;
> mind is their master, mind is their maker.
> Act or speak with an unwholesome state of mind,
> and suffering will follow
> as the cart-wheel follows the steps of the ox.

> All actions are led by the mind;
> mind is their master, mind is their maker.
> Act or speak with a pure state of mind,
> and happiness will follow
> as your shadow follows you without departing.

Hatred begets hatred. Loving-friendliness begets loving-friendliness. The Buddha practiced loving-friendliness in all directions, including toward himself.

When we have assimilated well true loving-friendliness, our actions are filled with metta. This falls into the category of right action in the noble eightfold path. Living from loving-friendliness, we naturally begin to abstain from killing, stealing, abusing senses, and lying.

CHAPTER 19

Cordiality and Loving-Friendliness

*W*hen monks in Kosamiya Village had a dispute, the Buddha compassionately advised them to practice the six factors of cordiality. The six factors are love, respect, cohesion, non-dispute, concord, and unity. These six factors are themselves deeply related to a life of loving-friendliness.

Speaking to his followers in Kosamiya, the Buddha asked them to practice these things:

1. Maintaining bodily acts of loving-friendliness in public and in private toward all companions in the holy life. The Buddha said: "This is a principle of cordiality that creates love and respect, and conduces to cohesion, to non-dispute, to concord, and to unity."

2. Maintaining verbal acts of loving-friendliness both in public and in private toward all companions in the holy life.

3. Maintaining mental acts of loving-friendliness both in public and in private toward all companions in the holy life.

4. Enjoying things in common with all virtuous companions in the holy life. The Buddha encouraged monks to share without reservations any gain of a kind that accords with the

Dharma and has been obtained in a way that accords with the Dharma—including even what is in a monk's bowl.

5. Maintaining both in public and in private virtues that are unbroken, untorn, unblotched, unmottled, liberating, commended by the wise, not misapprehended, and conducive to concentration. The Buddha also encouraged his followers to share these virtues with each other.

6. Maintaining in public and in private a holy life and right view that is noble and emancipating, and leads one to the complete destruction of suffering.

After giving this instruction to his followers, he turned to the monk Ananda and said, "These are the six principles of cordiality that create love and respect, and conduce to cohesion, to non-dispute, to concord, and to unity. If, Ananda, you undertake and maintain these six principles of cordiality, do you see any course of speech, trivial or gross, that you could not endure?"

"No, venerable sir," Ananda replied.

"Therefore, Ananda, undertake and maintain these six principles of cordiality. That will lead to your welfare and happiness for a long time."

It is said that Ananda was satisfied and delighted with the Buddha's words.

I encourage you to find ways you can integrate the six factors of cordiality into your own exploration of metta in your life.

CHAPTER 20

Listening, Speaking, and Working with Metta

*M*etta can be practiced in every aspect our life, in the little and big actions we engage in throughout our day and throughout our lives, and even in the simple acts of listening.

Sometimes people come to you to unload a heavy burden. If you have time, you can listen with metta. Just listening, you help them. Your attentive and patient listening might be all you can offer—but just that is actually a great and vast gift. Don't feel you have to have a solution to someone's problem, or answers, or a way to fix things. People often do not expect—or want!—a solution from you. They simply need someone to listen to them patiently. This is a metta practice in action.

Talking with metta can also relieve suffering. Sometimes conversations can turn into arguments. As soon as you realize that you are going to use verbal daggers against the other person, stop that train of thought. Then try to have your own personal, internal, and quiet dialogue for a short while. Ask yourself not to carry on the conversation the same way. Tell yourself that you have an "axe" that you were born with. That axe is your tongue. As it says in the *Sutta Nipata*, "At birth, an axe is born in a person's mouth. It destroys a foolish person who utters harmful words."

Sometimes you may see someone else in the process of becoming angry and upset. If you see an impending problem, by all means talk to the person who is going to get into trouble. If someone is already in trouble, spend time talking to him or her with metta in order to help. Even if someone is angry and behaving irrationally, you might be able to calm him or her with your words spoken from a place of loving-friendliness. Talking in such a way to agitated people slows them down, perhaps just a little, and helps them look at their mind with patience. You might prevent them from getting into further trouble.

We can train our eyes to look at people with metta. Seeing others with metta can prevent our own mind from forming a biased opinion. Looking at them with metta thoughts can prevent our own heart from forming false opinions of that person.

With metta in mind, we can transform even simple actions of everyday life into part of our practice of loving-friendliness. For instance, we can clean places to prevent dirt or foul smells from building up. Cleaning is a part of life, so why not do it with a spirit of loving-friendliness, and dedicate it to the well-being of others? Doing something to make others happy, even something simple, is a practice of metta.

If you are a cook, you can practice metta through your cooking. As you prepare your food, do it from a place of loving-friendliness. As you slice each carrot, repeat the metta phrases to yourself: "May this carrot bring peace to all who eat it. May all who eat this food be happy and safe."

Working physically to make others happy is a practice of metta. Doing community service is an act of metta. Helping neighbors, disabled people, or the destitute is a practice of loving-friendliness. Feeding the hungry is metta work. Educating the uneducated is metta work. Hospital service, hospice service, nursing care, and therapeutic exercises can be done with metta.

Helping others we help ourselves. There are so many things you can do in this world to help others that naturally arouse our own inner wonderful qualities. Everywhere in every society you find human beings who need help. If you do some work like that deliberately, your anger slowly fades away and you begin to appreciate life. You appreciate your own life and appreciate the lives of others. Effortlessly you can see many opportunities to practice metta. Just look around. You will find those opportunities.

One of the most beautiful things about loving-friendliness is that we develop our own metta practice by helping others with metta. When we practice metta our minds become calm and peaceful without hate. Seeing us calm, peaceful, and free from hate other people learn to practice metta. Then they too become calm and peaceful and free from hate. Without saying much we can influence others when we practice metta. This is one way that we help others by helping ourselves.

Suppose you want to teach a subject—say mathematics. You first must study mathematics and master it; then you can teach others mathematics. You learn how to swim; then you can teach others how to swim. You practice metta in thoughts, words, and deeds. Then you can teach others how to develop metta. Practicing metta for ourselves is deeply intertwined with practicing metta for others.

In the Dhammapada, the Buddha tells us:

> Don't give up your own welfare
> for the sake of theirs, however great.
> Clearly know your own welfare
> and be intent on the highest good.

In the *Great Discourse on Complete Liberation* (*Mahaparinibbana Sutta*), when the Buddha declared he was going to pass away in three months, the Venerable Ananda went to the Buddha's lodging. Leaning on the doorpost, he lamented, "I still have so much to learn, and the Teacher, who has been so compassionate with me, is passing away."

The Buddha replied, "Do not weep, Ananda. Have I not already told you that all things that are pleasant and delightful are changeable, subject to separation and taking on new forms? Since whatever is born is subject to decay, how could it be, Ananda, that I should not pass away? For a long time, Ananda, you have been in the Buddha's presence, showing loving-friendliness in every act of body, speech, and mind, beneficially, blessedly, wholeheartedly, and unstintingly. You have achieved much merit, Ananda. Make the effort, and in a short time you will be free."

These words of the Buddha were delivered with utmost loving-friendliness.

Ananda was comforted by the Buddha's last advice to him—and we should be too.

Some years ago, I arrived at London's Gatwick Airport several hours before my flight. Having time on my hands is a pleasure for me, since it means more opportunity for meditation. So, after checking in and seeing the location of the gate, I sat cross-legged with my eyes closed on an airport bench. I filled my mind with thoughts of loving-friendliness for everyone, everywhere, trying to permeate my whole being with love.

Absorbed in feelings of loving-friendliness in that busy airport, I felt two tiny, tender hands reaching around my neck. I opened my eyes slowly and discovered a little girl with blue eyes and blond, curly locks, perhaps two years old, hugging me. Then I looked over and saw her mother chasing after her. Her mother asked me, "Please bless my little girl and let her go." So I said to the child, "Please go back to your mother. Your mother has lots of kisses for you, lots of hugs, lots of toys, and lots of sweets. I have none of those things. Please go."

The child continued to hang on to my neck, and she wouldn't let go. The mother folded her palms together and pleaded with me in a kindly tone, "Please, sir, give her your blessing and let her go." By this time, others were beginning to gather. And again, I urged the little girl, "Please go back to your mother. You and your mother have a plane to catch. You are late. Your mother has all your toys and candy. I have nothing. Please go to her." But she still wouldn't budge. Finally, the mother gently took the little girl's hands off my neck and asked me once again to bless her. "You are a very good little girl," I said. "Your mother loves you very much. Hurry, you might miss your plane."

Perhaps the child was intrigued by my robes; maybe she thought I was Santa Claus or a fairy-tale figure. But there is another possibility: I was sitting on that bench practicing metta, sending out thoughts of loving-friendliness with every breath, through every pore of my being. Perhaps she felt the energy. Children can be extremely sensitive; they sense whatever feelings are around them. She may have been drawn to the feeling of loving-friendliness.

We should never underestimate what effect the example we set may have on others—especially the young, who are beginning to learn how to be in the world. When I was living at the Washington Buddhist Vihara I got to know a little boy, a seven-year-old neighbor. Sometimes we would walk the Vihara grounds together. He was very kind toward me and one time even said, "I wish I had a brother like you." One day when he and I were walking he saw a grasshopper. He quietly approached him and tried to crush it, saying, "You miserable creature!"

I said, "No, no, don't crush him. Let him go. If you crush him I will be very sad." Seeing another's perspective showed him a different way of being with others—in this case, how to treat an insect with loving-friendliness. He apologized to me and stopped trying to crush the grasshopper. He continued to come to the Vihara until he and his parents moved away from that area.

There is no wrong time to give someone our loving attention, and no time too soon. One day when I was leading a retreat, a young pregnant woman came forward with a question in a group interview. She asked when she should teach her child metta meditation. I said, "Now is a good time. When you practice loving-friendliness now, your baby feels peace and will develop a healthy, peaceful mind. In the womb your baby will feel all your emotions—negative or positive. After the birth go on practicing metta while breastfeeding. As the baby grows, keep the baby with you when you meditate. As you keep your child next to you when you meditate the child may sleep peacefully and wake up peacefully. Your child grows peacefully with a very healthy mind."

After the interview another young woman came and thanked me for blessing her pregnant sister with my reply. Her three-year-old nephew straightaway came up to me and hugged me, putting his hands around my neck. Everyone needs our loving-friendliness—all beings want to be cared for and appreciated. And because of this, we can encourage others by our example, our own practice—and even our gratitude. For instance, when we see people doing any good thing we can practice metta by thanking them and encouraging them to do similar good things. Sometimes this goodwill returns to us, other times it is passed on to strangers. These good actions then spread out like ripples on the water, endlessly.

Make the effort to practice loving-friendliness in the entirety of your life. And in short time, you will be free!

The Buddha's Discourses on Loving-Friendliness

The Buddha delivered two sermons specifically on loving-friendliness, and both are commonly referred to as the *Metta Sutta*. One is the *Discourse on the Benefits of Loving-Friendliness* (*Metta Nisamsa Sutta*), and the other is the *Discourse on Loving-Friendliness* (*Karaniya Metta Sutta*), which has been the main subject of this book. You can recite either or both of these teachings of the Buddha to help cultivate the energy of loving-friendliness.

The word *sutta* derives from the Indo-European root word for "suture." It is a thread that binds the teachings together. More than ten thousand suttas have been collected in the Pali language. These are the earliest record of the Buddha's teachings. They were recalled by the Buddha's attendant, Ananda, and passed on for generations before being committed to writing. It is Ananda who says in these verses, "Thus have I heard."

These discourses are often memorized in traditional monastic training. While we may not have to memorize the whole discourse, even if we recite one sentence with metta in our heart, like "May all beings be well, happy, and peaceful," we can start to overcome our anger and fill the mind with peace.

Let us do this with utmost sincerity.

DISCOURSE ON THE BENEFITS OF LOVING-FRIENDLINESS
(Metta Nisamsa Sutta)

Thus have I heard. At one time, when the Blessed One was living near Savatthi at Jetavana at Anathapindika's monastery, he addressed the monks saying, "O Monks."

"Yes, venerable sir," the monks replied.

The Blessed One then spoke as follows: "O Monks, there are eleven benefits from loving-friendliness that arise from the emancipation of the heart; if repeated, developed, made much of, made a habit of, made a basis of, experienced, practiced, well started, these eleven benefits are expected.

"What are the eleven?

1. One sleeps well.
2. One gets up well.
3. One does not have nightmares.
4. One becomes affectionate to human beings.
5. One becomes affectionate to non-human beings.
6. The deities protect one.
7. Neither fire nor poison nor weapon affect one.
8. One's mind becomes calm immediately.
9. One's complexion brightens.
10. One dies without confusion.
11. Beyond that, if one does not comprehend the highest, one goes to the world of the brahmas.

"O Monks, there are eleven benefits from loving-friendliness that arise from the emancipation of the heart; if repeated, developed, made much of, made a habit of, made a basis of, experienced, practiced, well started, these eleven benefits are expected."

Thus spoke the Exalted One. Delighted, the monks rejoiced in what the Exalted One had said.

DISCOURSE ON LOVING-FRIENDLINESS
(Karaniya Metta Sutta)

Thus have I heard. At one time when the Blessed One was living near Savatthi at Jetavana at Anathapindika's monastery, he addressed the monks saying, "Monks."

"Venerable sir," the monks replied.

The Blessed One then spoke as follows:

"This is what should be done
By one who is skilled in goodness,
And who knows the path of peace:
Let them be able and upright,
Straightforward and gentle in speech.
Humble and not conceited,
Contented and easily satisfied.
Unburdened with duties and frugal in their ways.
Peaceful and calm, and wise and skillful,
Not proud and demanding in nature.
Let them not do the slightest thing
That the wise would later reprove.
Wishing: In gladness and in safety,
May all beings be at ease.
Whatever living beings there may be;
Whether they are weak or strong, omitting none,
The great or the mighty, medium, short or small,
The seen and the unseen,
Those living near and far away,
Those born and to-be-born,
May all beings be at ease!

Let none deceive another,
Or despise any being in any state.
Let none through anger or ill will
Wish harm upon another.
Even as a mother protects with her life
Her child, her only child,
So with a boundless heart
Should one cherish all beings:
Radiating kindness over the entire world
Spreading upwards to the skies,
And downwards to the depths;
Outwards and unbounded,
Freed from hatred and ill will.

Whether standing or walking, seated or lying down,
Free from drowsiness,
One should sustain this recollection.
This is said to be the sublime abiding.
By not holding to fixed views,
The pure-hearted one, having clarity of vision,
Being freed from all sense desires,
Is not born again into this world."

Loving-Friendliness Meditations

*A*s discussed in chapter 3, there are several methods you can use to cultivate loving-friendliness. Metta meditation lays the groundwork for the development of loving-friendliness. There are several varieties of meditation. Among all, repetition is key. Whether you are repeating words from a sutta, consistently setting aside time for meditation, or simply mentally returning to feelings of warm-heartedness during your day, making loving-friendliness a habit will help you cultivate it over time. Though the change may be imperceptible from one session to the next, with regular practice meditation on loving-friendliness may have a significant effect on your life and your relationships with others.

General Instructions

The following are a few meditations you may use as a script for your loving-friendliness meditation. As a beginner, find a quiet place to sit and spend ample time with one of these meditations. Slowly read it over and allow yourself to feel loving-friendliness radiate out from your heart as described. In this meditation, we start with the words and ideas. These words are a suggestion—you may choose some variant of one of these or add to it in a way that is meaningful for you.

Start with yourself as the focal point of the meditation, and extend your peace and good wishes outward until it includes all beings in the universe. You may find it helpful to imagine specific people or animals at each stage. Hold them in your mind and sincerely feel loving-friendliness for all beings. If some category of being is challenging for you, be patient and earnest in your meditation until it feels fluid.

Focus on the physical feelings that arise until they become a pure distillation of all your thoughts and physical sensations. It is a feeling beyond sensation, almost an emotional coloring in the mind. It is often accompanied by sensations of warmth and swelling in the area of the heart.

As you gradually become more comfortable with this meditation, drop the words and images, the beings, and stages. Move deeply into metta as an intangible thing—beyond thought, emotion, and physical feeling.

In due course, outside of formal meditation practice these words will come back to you when you need them most. Let metta become second nature.

MEDITATION 1

May I be well, happy, and peaceful. May no harm come to me. May I always meet with spiritual success. May I also have patience, courage, understanding, and determination to meet and overcome inevitable difficulties, problems, and failures in life. May I always rise above them with morality, integrity, forgiveness, compassion, mindfulness, and wisdom.

May my parents be well, happy, and peaceful. May no harm come to them. May they always meet with spiritual success. May they also have patience, courage, understanding, and determination to meet and overcome inevitable difficulties, problems, and failures in life. May they always rise above them with morality, integrity, forgiveness, compassion, mindfulness, and wisdom.

May my teachers be well, happy, and peaceful. May no harm come to them. May they always meet with spiritual success. May they also have patience, courage, understanding, and determination to meet and overcome inevitable difficulties, problems, and failures in life. May they always rise above them with morality, integrity, forgiveness, compassion, mindfulness, and wisdom.

May my relatives be well, happy, and peaceful. May no harm come to them. May they always meet with spiritual success. May they also have patience, courage, understanding, and determination to meet and overcome inevitable difficulties, problems, and failures in life. May they always rise above them with morality, integrity, forgiveness, compassion, mindfulness, and wisdom.

May my friends be well, happy, and peaceful. May no harm come to them. May they always meet with spiritual success. May they also have patience, courage, understanding, and determination to meet and overcome inevitable difficulties, problems, and failures in life. May they always rise above them with morality, integrity, forgiveness, compassion, mindfulness, and wisdom.

May all indifferent persons be well, happy, and peaceful. May no harm come to them. May they always meet with spiritual success. May they also have patience, courage, understanding, and determination to meet and overcome inevitable difficulties, problems, and failures in life. May they always rise above them with morality, integrity, forgiveness, compassion, mindfulness, and wisdom.

May all unfriendly persons be well, happy, and peaceful. May no harm come to them. May they always meet with spiritual success. May they also have patience, courage, understanding, and determination to meet and overcome inevitable difficulties, problems, and failures in life. May they always rise above them with morality, integrity, forgiveness, compassion, mindfulness, and wisdom.

May all living beings be well, happy, and peaceful. May no harm come to them. May they always meet with spiritual success. May they also have patience, courage, understanding, and determination to meet and overcome inevitable difficulties, problems, and failures in life. May they always rise above them with morality, integrity, forgiveness, compassion, mindfulness, and wisdom.

MEDITATION 2

Having seen that all beings, like myself, have a desire for happiness, I should methodically develop loving-friendliness toward all beings.

May I be happy and free from suffering.

And always, like myself, may my friends, neutral persons, and the hostile be happy too.

May all beings in this village, in this state, in other countries, and in all world systems be ever happy.

So too may all women, men, noble ones, non-noble ones, gods, humans, and beings in the lower worlds be happy.

May all beings in the ten directions be happy.

May I be free from hatred. May I be free from affliction. May I be free from worry. May I live happily. As I am, so also may my parents, teachers, preceptors, and friendly, indifferent, and hostile beings be free from hatred. May they be free from affliction. May they be free from worry. May they live happily. May they be released from suffering. May they not be deprived of their fortune, duly acquired.

May all beings…

May all living things…

May all creatures…

May all persons…

May all women…

May all men…

May all noble ones…

May all non-noble ones…

May all gods…

May all humans…

May all non-humans…

May all those who are in the hell realms…

May all those who are in this home…

May all those who are in this town…

May all those who are in this country…

May all those who are in this world…

May all those who are in this galaxy…

May all of them, without any exception, be free from worry. May they live happily. May they be released from suffering. May they not be deprived of their fortune, duly acquired.

May those with no feet receive my love. May those with two feet receive my love. May those with four feet receive my love. May those with many feet receive my love.

May those with no feet not hurt me. May those with two feet not hurt me. May those with four feet not hurt me. May those with many feet not hurt me.

May all beings, all those with life, all who have become, all in their entirety—may all see what is good. May suffering not come to anyone.

May those who suffer be free from suffering. May the fear-struck be free from fear. May those who grieve be free from grief, so too may all beings be.

From the highest realm of existence to the lowest, may all beings arisen in these realms, with form and without form, with perception and without perception, be released from all suffering and attain perfect peace.

MEDITATION 3

May my mind be filled with the thought of loving-friendliness, compassion, appreciative joy, and equanimity. May I be generous. May I be gentle. May I be grateful. May I be relaxed. May I be happy and peaceful. May

I be healthy. May my heart become soft. May my words be pleasing to others.

May all that I see, hear, smell, taste, touch, and think help me to cultivate loving-friendliness, compassion, appreciative joy, equanimity, generosity, and gentleness. May my behavior be friendly and my loving-friendliness be a source of peace and happiness. May my behavior help my personality. May I be free from fear, tension, anxiety, worry, and restlessness.

Wherever I go in the world, may I meet people with happiness, peace, and friendliness. May I be protected in all directions from greed, anger, aversion, hatred, jealousy, and fear.

May the minds of my parents be filled with the thought of loving-friendliness, compassion, appreciative joy, and equanimity. May they be generous. May they be gentle. May they be grateful. May they be relaxed. May they be happy and peaceful. May they be healthy. May their hearts become soft. May their words be pleasing to others.

May all that my parents see, hear, smell, taste, touch, and think help them to cultivate loving-friendliness, compassion, appreciative joy, equanimity, generosity, and gentleness. May their behavior be friendly and their loving-friendliness be a source of peace and happiness. May this behavior help their personalities. May they be free from fear, tension, anxiety, worry, and restlessness.

Wherever they go in the world, may they meet people with happiness, peace, and friendliness. May they be protected in all directions from greed, anger, aversion, hatred, jealousy, and fear.

May the minds of my teachers be filled with the thought of loving-friendliness, compassion, appreciative joy, and equanimity. May they be generous. May they be gentle. May they be grateful. May they be relaxed. May they be happy and peaceful. May they be healthy. May their hearts become soft. May their words be pleasing to others.

May all that my teachers see, hear, smell, taste, touch, and think help them to cultivate loving-friendliness, compassion, appreciative joy, equanimity, generosity, and gentleness. May their behavior be friendly and their loving-friendliness be a source of peace and happiness. May this behavior help their personalities. May all of them be free from fear, tension, anxiety, worry, and restlessness.

Wherever they go in the world, may they meet people with happiness, peace, and friendliness. May they be protected in all directions from greed, anger, aversion, hatred, jealousy, and fear.

May the minds of my relatives be filled with the thought of loving-friendliness, compassion, appreciative joy, and equanimity. May they be generous. May they be gentle. May they be grateful. May they be relaxed. May they be happy and peaceful. May they be healthy. May their hearts become soft. May their words be pleasing to others.

May all that my relatives see, hear, smell, taste, touch, and think help them to cultivate loving-friendliness, compassion, appreciative joy, equanimity, generosity, and gentleness. May their behavior be friendly and their loving-friendliness be a source of peace and happiness. May this behavior help their personalities. May all of them be free from fear, tension, anxiety, worry, and restlessness.

Wherever they go in the world, may they meet people with happiness, peace, and friendliness. May they be protected in all directions from greed, anger, aversion, hatred, jealousy, and fear.

May the minds of my friends be filled with the thought of loving-friendliness, compassion, appreciative joy, and equanimity. May they be generous. May they be gentle. May they be grateful. May they be relaxed. May they be happy and peaceful. May they be healthy. May their hearts become soft. May their words be pleasing to others.

May all that my friends see, hear, smell, taste, touch, and think help them to cultivate loving-friendliness, compassion, appreciative joy, equanimity, generosity, and gentleness. May their behavior be friendly and their loving-friendliness be a source of peace and happiness. May this behavior help their personalities. May all of them be free from fear, tension, anxiety, worry, and restlessness.

Wherever they go in the world, may they meet people with happiness, peace, and friendliness. May they be protected in all directions from greed, anger, aversion, hatred, jealousy, and fear.

May the minds of all indifferent persons be filled with the thought of loving-friendliness, compassion, appreciative joy, equanimity. May they be generous. May they be gentle. May they be grateful. May they be relaxed. May they be happy and peaceful. May they be healthy. May their hearts become soft. May their words be pleasing to others.

May everything that all indifferent persons see, hear, smell, taste, touch, and think help them to cultivate loving-friendliness, compassion, appreciative joy, equanimity, generosity, and gentleness. May their behavior be friendly and their loving-friendliness be a source of peace and happiness. May this behavior help their personalities. May all of them be free from fear, tension, anxiety, worry, and restlessness.

Wherever they go in the world, may they meet people with happiness, peace, and friendliness. May they be protected in all directions from greed, anger, aversion, hatred, jealousy, and fear.

May the minds of all unfriendly persons be filled with the thought of loving-friendliness, compassion, appreciative joy, and equanimity. May they be generous. May they be gentle. May they be grateful. May they be relaxed. May they be happy and peaceful. May they be healthy. May their hearts become soft. May their words be pleasing to others.

May everything that all unfriendly persons see, hear, smell, taste, touch, and think help them to cultivate loving-friendliness, compassion, appreciative joy, equanimity, generosity, and gentleness. May their behavior be friendly and their loving-friendliness be a source of peace and happiness. May this behavior help their personalities. May all of them be free from fear, tension, anxiety, worry, and restlessness.

Wherever they go in the world, may they meet people with happiness, peace, and friendliness. May they be protected in all directions from greed, anger, aversion, hatred, jealousy, and fear.

May the minds of all living beings be filled with the thought of loving-friendliness, compassion, appreciative joy, and equanimity. May they be generous. May they be gentle. May they be grateful. May they be relaxed. May they be happy and peaceful. May they be healthy. May their hearts become soft. May their words be pleasing to others.

May everything that all living beings see, hear, smell, taste, touch, and think help them to cultivate loving-friendliness, compassion, appreciative joy, equanimity, generosity, and gentleness. May their behavior be friendly and their loving-friendliness be a source of peace and happiness. May this behavior help their personalities. May all of them be free from fear, tension, anxiety, worry, and restlessness.

Wherever they go in the world, may they meet people with happiness, peace, and friendliness. May they be protected in all directions from greed, anger, aversion, hatred, jealousy, and fear.

MEDITATION 4

Let us direct our minds in the eastern direction and wish that all living beings in that direction be free from greed, anger, aversion, hatred, jealousy, and fear. Let these thoughts of loving-friendliness embrace all of them, envelop them. Let every cell, every drop of blood, every atom, every molecule of their entire bodies and minds be charged with these thoughts of loving-friendliness. Let their bodies and minds be relaxed and filled with the peace and tranquility of loving-friendliness. Let the peace and tranquility of loving-friendliness pervade their entire bodies and minds.

Let us direct our minds to the southern direction and wish that all living beings in that direction be free from greed, anger, aversion, hatred, jealousy, and fear. Let these thoughts of loving-friendliness embrace all of them, envelop them. Let every cell, every drop of blood, every atom, every molecule of their entire bodies and minds be charged with these thoughts of loving-friendliness. Let their bodies and minds be relaxed and filled with the peace and tranquility of loving-friendliness. Let the peace and tranquility of loving-friendliness pervade their entire bodies and minds.

Let us direct our minds to the western direction and wish that all living beings in that direction be free from greed, anger, aversion, hatred, jealousy, and fear. Let these thoughts of loving-friendliness embrace all of them, envelop them. Let every cell, every drop of blood, every atom, every molecule of their entire bodies and minds be charged with these thoughts of loving-friendliness. Let their bodies and minds be relaxed and filled with the peace and tranquility of loving-friendliness. Let the peace and tranquility of loving-friendliness pervade their entire bodies and minds.

Let us direct our minds to the northern direction and wish that all living beings in that direction be free from greed, anger, aversion, hatred, jealousy, and fear. Let these thoughts of loving-friendliness embrace all of them, envelop them. Let every cell, every drop of blood, every atom, every molecule of their entire bodies and minds be charged with these thoughts of loving-friendliness. Let their bodies and minds be relaxed and filled with the peace and tranquility of loving-friendliness. Let the peace and tranquility of loving-friendliness pervade their entire bodies and minds.

Let us direct our minds to the celestial direction and wish that all living beings in that direction be free from greed, anger, aversion, hatred, jealousy, and fear. Let these thoughts of loving-friendliness embrace all of them, envelop them. Let every cell, every drop of blood, every atom, every molecule of their entire bodies and minds be charged with these thoughts of loving-friendliness. Let their bodies and minds be relaxed and filled with the peace and tranquility of loving-friendliness. Let the peace and tranquility of loving-friendliness pervade their entire bodies and minds.

Let us direct our minds to the animal realm and hell realms and wish that all living beings in that direction be free from greed, anger, aversion, hatred, jealousy, and fear. Let these thoughts of loving-friendliness embrace all of them, envelop them. Let every cell, every drop of blood, every atom, every molecule of their entire bodies and minds be charged with these thoughts of loving-friendliness. Let their bodies and minds be relaxed and filled with the peace and tranquility of loving-friendliness. Let the peace and tranquility of loving-friendliness pervade their entire bodies and minds.

May all beings in all directions, all around the universe, be beautiful; let them be happy; let them have good fortune; let them have good friends; let them after death be reborn in heavens.

May all beings everywhere be filled with the feeling of loving-friendliness, abundant, exalted, measureless, free from enmity, free from affliction and anxiety. May they live happily.

May all those who are imprisoned legally or illegally, all who are in police custody anywhere in the world awaiting trials, be met with peace and happiness. May they be free from greed, anger, aversion, hatred, jealousy, and fear. Let these thoughts of loving-friendliness embrace all of them, envelop them. Let every cell, every drop of blood, every atom, every molecule of their entire bodies and minds be charged with these thoughts of friendliness. Let their bodies and minds be relaxed and filled with the peace and tranquility of loving-friendliness. Let the peace and tranquility of loving-friendliness pervade their entire bodies and minds.

May all of them in all directions, all around the universe, be beautiful; let them be happy; let them have good fortune; let them have good friends; let them after death be reborn in heavens.

May all who are in hospitals suffering from numerous sicknesses be met with peace and happiness. May they be free from pain, afflictions, depression, disappointment, dissatisfaction, anxiety, and fear. Let these thoughts of loving-friendliness embrace all of them, envelop them. Let every cell, every drop of blood, every atom, every molecule of their entire bodies and minds be charged with these thoughts of friendliness. Let their bodies and minds be relaxed and filled with the peace and tranquility of loving-friendliness. Let the peace and tranquility of loving-friendliness pervade their entire bodies and minds.

May all of them in all directions, all around the universe, be beautiful; let them be happy; let them have good fortune; let them have good friends; let them after death be reborn in heavens.

May all mothers who are in pain delivering babies be met with peace and happiness. May they be free from pain, afflictions, depression, disappointment, dissatisfaction, anxiety, and fear. Let these thoughts of loving-friendliness embrace all of them, envelop them. Let every cell, every drop of blood, every atom, every molecule of their entire bodies and minds be charged with these thoughts of friendliness. Let their bodies and minds be relaxed and filled with the peace and tranquility of loving-friendliness. Let the peace and tranquility of loving-friendliness pervade their entire bodies and minds.

May all of them in all directions, all around the universe, be beautiful; let them be happy; let them have good fortune; let them have good friends; let them after death be reborn in heavens.

May all single parents taking care of their children be free from pain, afflictions, depression, disappointment, dissatisfaction, anxiety, and fear. Let these thoughts of loving-friendliness embrace all of them, envelop them. Let every cell, every drop of blood, every atom, every molecule of their entire bodies and minds be charged with these thoughts of friendliness. Let their bodies and minds be relaxed and filled with the peace and tranquility of loving-friendliness. Let the peace and tranquility of loving-friendliness pervade their entire bodies and minds.

May all of them in all directions, all around the universe, be beautiful; let them be happy; let them have good fortune; let them have good friends; let them after death be reborn in heavens.

May all children abused by adults in numerous ways be free from pain, afflictions, depression, disappointment, dissatisfaction, anxiety, and fear. Let these thoughts of loving-friendliness embrace all of them, envelop them. Let every cell, every drop of blood, every atom, every molecule of their entire bodies and minds be charged with these thoughts of friendliness. Let their bodies and minds be relaxed and filled with the peace and tranquility of loving-friendliness. Let the peace and tranquility of loving-friendliness pervade their entire bodies and minds.

May all of them in all directions, all around the universe, be beautiful; let them be happy; let them have good fortune; let them have good friends; let them after death be reborn in heavens.

May all leaders be gentle, kind, generous, compassionate, considerate, and have the best understanding of the oppressed, underprivileged, discriminated-against, and poverty-stricken. May their hearts melt at the suffering of the unfortunate citizens. May the oppressed, underprivileged, discriminated-against, and poverty-stricken be free from pain, afflictions, depression, disappointment, dissatisfaction, anxiety, and fear. Let these thoughts of loving-friendliness embrace all of them, envelop them. Let every cell, every drop of blood, every atom, every molecule of their entire bodies and minds be charged with these thoughts of friendliness. Let their bodies and minds be relaxed and filled with the peace and tranquility of loving-friendliness. Let the peace and tranquility of loving-friendliness pervade their entire bodies and minds.

May all of them in all directions, all around the universe, be beautiful; let them be happy; let them have good fortune; let them have good friends; let them after death be reborn in heavens.

Index

About the Author

*B*hante Henepola Gunaratana was ordained as a Buddhist monk at the age of twelve in Malandeniya, Sri Lanka. He's the author of *Mindfulness in Plain English, Eight Mindful Steps to Happiness,* and several more books—including his autobiography, *Journey to Mindfulness.* He travels and teaches throughout the world and currently lives at Bhavana Society Forest Monastery in West Virginia.

What to Read Next
by Bhante Gunaratana
from Wisdom Publications

Mindfulness in Plain English

"A classic—one of the very best English sources for authoritative explanations of mindfulness."
—Daniel Goleman, author of *Emotional Intelligence*

Beyond Mindfulness in Plain English
An Introductory Guide to Deeper States of Meditation

"A straightforward and pragmatic guide to deepening levels of concentration and insight. This book is a joy to read and a great gift to us all."
—Joseph Goldstein, author of *Mindfulness*

The Four Foundations of Mindfulness in Plain English

"The Four Foundations come to life. Drink long, drink deeply."
—Jon Kabat-Zinn, author of *Wherever You Go, There You Are*

Eight Mindful Steps to Happiness
Walking the Buddha's Path

"Bhante Gunaratana's forte is his presentation of clear, intelligent insight into the most basic teaching. This is another exceptional example of how profound a simple and accessible book can be."
—*Tricycle: The Buddhist Review*

Meditation on Perception
Ten Healing Practices to Cultivate Mindfulness

"Clear and concise, this book is invaluable."
—Toni Bernhard, author of *How to Be Sick*

Journey to Mindfulness
The Autobiography of Bhante G.
with Jeanne Malmgren

"This plain-English look back at seventy-five years of an admixture of adversity, humility, and hard-won wisdom tells an engaging story that non-Buddhists can appreciate as well as Buddhists."
—*Publishers Weekly*

Start Here, Start Now
A Short Guide to Meditation

"A timeless, clear, and beautiful introduction."
—Tamara Levitt, Head of Mindfulness at Calm

What, Why, How
Answers to Your Questions About Buddhism, Meditation, and Living Mindfully

"This book can be of help to anyone's spiritual journey and meditation practice."
—Sharon Salzberg, author of *Lovingkindness and Real Happiness*